Get the Job You Really Want

James Caan is one of the UK's most successful and dynamic entrepreneurs, and has been building and selling businesses since 1985.

After dropping out of school at sixteen and starting his first business in a Pall Mall broom cupboard, armed with little more than charm and his father's advice, Caan went on to make his fortune in the recruitment industry, founding the Alexander Mann Group, which grew to a turnover of £130 million. He also co-founded executive headhunting firm Humana International, growing it to 147 offices across thirty countries in six years.

Caan graduated from Harvard Business School in 2003, and went on to set up private equity firm Hamilton Bradshaw. Based in Mayfair, Hamilton Bradshaw specializes in buyouts, venture capital and turnarounds in the recruitment sector, as well as real estate investments and development opportunities in both the UK and Europe.

A winner of PriceWaterhouseCoopers Entrepreneur of the Year and BT Enterprise of the Year award, Caan joined the panel of the BBC's *Dragons' Den* in 2007. He is a regular in the national and business press, he advises various government programmes, and he initiates philanthropic projects via the James Caan Foundation.

Get the Job You Really Want

James Caan

PORTFOLIO
PENGUIN

PORTFOLIO PENGUIN

Published by the Penguin Group
Penguin Books Ltd, 80 Strand, London WC2R ORL, England
Penguin Group (USA) Inc., 375 Hudson Street, New York, New York 10014, USA
Penguin Group (Canada), 90 Eglinton Avenue East, Suite 700, Toronto, Ontario, Canada M4P 2Y3
(a division of Pearson Penguin Canada Inc.)
Penguin Ireland, 25 St Stephen's Green, Dublin 2, Ireland
(a division of Penguin Books Ltd)
Penguin Group (Australia), 250 Camberwell Road, Camberwell, Victoria 3124, Australia
(a division of Pearson Australia Group Pty Ltd)
Penguin Books India Pvt Ltd, 11 Community Centre, Panchsheel Park, New Delhi – 110 017, India
Penguin Group (NZ), 67 Apollo Drive, Rosedale, North Shore 0632, New Zealand
(a division of Pearson New Zealand Ltd)
Penguin Books (South Africa) (Pty) Ltd, 24 Sturdee Avenue, Rosebank, Johannesburg 2196, South Africa

Penguin Books Ltd, Registered Offices: 80 Strand, London WC2R ORL, England

www.penguin.com

First published 2011
4

Copyright © James Caan, Philip Dodd, 2011
All rights reserved

The moral right of the authors has been asserted

Set in TheMix and Trade Gothic
Designed and typeset by Richard Marston
Printed in Great Britain by Clays Ltd, St Ives plc

ISBN 978-0-670-91940-6

www.greenpenguin.co.uk

Penguin Books is committed to a sustainable future
for our business, our readers and our planet.
The book in your hands is made from paper
certified by the Forest Stewardship Council.

'It's your attitude not your aptitude that determines your altitude.'

Contents

INTRODUCTION

A couple of years ago, I ran an advertisement for an investment manager at my private equity company, Hamilton Bradshaw. In the advert we said the successful candidate had to have three years' chartered accounting experience, must have worked for one of the top five accounting firms, and should be Oxbridge educated or the equivalent. It was the standard specification for the job.

Early one afternoon I got a call from reception. 'I've got somebody downstairs who wants to see you.'

I took a quick look at my diary and saw I didn't have any appointments listed in my schedule. 'I'm sorry,' I said, 'I can't see anybody. I'm too busy right now,' and put the phone down.

Forty-five minutes later, there was another call. 'James, he's still sitting in reception.'

'What's it about?'

'Oh, he said he just wants to see James Caan.'

'No, forget it.' Nevertheless I did ask one of my team to pop downstairs and explain that we never do random appointments, and to say sorry, but there were no free slots available. While he went off to convey the message, I got on with the work I was doing.

Unknown to me, even after having been given the bad news, the guy in reception had simply asked what time the office closed, and carried on sitting there, waiting patiently. It happened that I had a meeting in the City later that afternoon, and at four o'clock I came out through reception and left the building.

Suddenly I sensed somebody behind me. I turned round to hear, 'Hi, James. My name's Greg. I saw your advert for an investment manager, and although I don't have any of the qualifications you're asking for, I know I can do the job.'

I looked at this guy and couldn't help smiling, because even while I was thinking to myself, 'What a cheek!' I had to admire the fact he had worked out that, since he didn't have either the right degree or the relevant experience, this was the only way he was ever going to get hold of me.

So I said, 'My car's parked round the corner. You have exactly one minute until I get to my car to tell me why you think I should give you an interview. Sixty seconds, starting from now.'

Greg gave me the pitch of his life – essentially telling me that although he lacked the specific academic qualifications, and hadn't worked for a top accounting firm, in practical terms he *had* done the job. 'I'm determined,' he insisted. 'I'm hardworking. I've read your website. I know the business you're in.

I know exactly what you do, and I understand the concept of how you manage portfolios.'

Because of all the research he had done, Greg knew so much about the company and our business that at the end of his one-minute spiel, I had to say, 'OK, here's my investment director's phone number. Give him a call. We're all out at a meeting until eight o'clock this evening, but if you call him then, I'll make sure you get an appointment.'

Bang on the dot of 8 p.m. he phoned the investment director. We invited him in for an interview. Normally I would never attend a first interview but this time I did, along with our investment director and our chief investment officer. Beforehand I had decided I was going to give Greg an *extremely* hard time. He had pushed himself into contention by showing plenty of nerve. I felt that if he was that self-confident about his own abilities, he had better be seriously good. We gave him a really tough interview, and asked some very searching, probing questions. I was amazed. He came back with a great answer to every question. Talk about resilient!

At the end of the interview, I asked Greg to wait outside while I had a chat with my colleagues. The three of us agreed we should give him the job there and then. We all realized that we could have interviewed somebody who had all the qualifications, but what value could we put on sheer determination, drive and hunger for the job?

We brought him back in and said, 'To our astonishment, we are delighted to offer you the position.' Greg joined us, and performed really well in the company. By thinking outside the box, and turning the usual conventions upside down, he had landed his ideal job.

This book is about precisely that: how to get the job you really want and transform your career. At a time when the only thing in business that seems certain is uncertainty, and the job market is as challenging as it's ever been, I am going to give you the best advice I can, based on thirty years of experience working in, setting up and running recruitment companies.

It's a battle royal out there in the job market, so you need all the ammunition you can get to give you an extra edge and to make a real difference.

I will take you through the whole process step by step. How to remain positive in a difficult economic climate. How to be proactive in finding the right job opportunities. How to go about packaging yourself to make sure you secure an interview. The vital importance of preparation, so that you are relaxed and confident in the interview, and can give a great performance. How to close the deal on a job offer to your best advantage. And at every stage I will try to shed a different light on the traditional, formulaic ways of approaching the whole process.

This is a time for flexibility and imagination. But you also need to put in the hard work – just as Greg had done in researching Hamilton Bradshaw so thoroughly (although, just in case you're thinking of pitching up in reception to try and ambush me in the way he did, that was definitely a one-off!). Unbelievably, ninety-five per cent of candidates never bother to go that extra mile. Nobody has ever told them how to go about getting a job. They just do what's instinctive. They see a job ad and, almost without thinking, send out their old CV and keep their fingers crossed.

I can only say this because I have been working in recruitment all my life. I didn't just stumble across this knowledge. I have learned the ins and outs and the details of the business from personal, hands-on experience. Together we are going to set about improving the odds of you getting that perfect job.

Because I really do believe that it is possible to have the job of your dreams. But you have got to be capable of doing it. There's no point in saying, 'I want to be Prime Minister,' for example, if you can't do the job. You will only be able to perform in a role if you have the skills to do it, but landing it is about planning, preparation and determination. Remember that most people, the vast majority of the other candidates who are applying for the job you want, do not even attempt ten per cent of the extra work that would make a significant difference to their chances. And that is why they are not in those jobs.

A great way to motivate yourself is to take inspiration from somebody you admire who has got their ideal job through commitment, belief and real drive. I look at people like Stuart Rose, who started off at Marks and Spencer as a management trainee in the early 1970s and thirty years later was appointed chief executive of the company. Philip Clarke, a Saturday boy at Tesco when he was fourteen, who went on to take over as chief executive of the company from Terry Leahy, who'd also stacked shelves in a Tesco store as a kid. Or Rose Marie Bravo, who was a buyer in a Long Island department store, and ended up running Saks Fifth Avenue before turning the fortunes of Burberry around.

And what better inspiration than Barack Obama? Look at where he came from and where he is today. He had to believe in himself – and what were the odds *against* him getting that job? To borrow his catchphrase: Can you get the job of your dreams? Yes, you can. Absolutely.

There are many people out there who have broken the mould, who have crossed the line, who have believed in themselves enough to get the job they really wanted. But what you have to bear in mind is that none of them chanced upon those jobs. They earned the right to have them. This book is not about hoping you get lucky. It is about creating your own luck.

Get the Job
You Really Want

"Yes, the job market is tougher than ever. Yes, competition for jobs is ferocious. But this could be the perfect opportunity for you to prove your real value."

1. POSITIVITY

You might be forgiven for thinking that trying to find the job of
your dreams in the middle of a turbulent economic climate –
the most severe downturn we have seen in three generations
– would be the worst of all possible times.

It is true that the employment market has been under stress.
Redundancy and unemployment figures have risen back to
levels not seen since the recession of the 1990s. There are few
sectors which have been unaffected, and many people are, not
surprisingly, worried about the uncertainty of the job market.

Private companies are tightening their belts to stay afloat,
and the public sector is having its budgets slashed – and in both
cases that always means staff numbers are culled, because
reducing headcount and salary bills is always an easy option.
The concept of a 'job for life' is long gone. Unemployment is
rising, and the official figure doesn't include those people who
would like to change jobs but are desperately hanging on to

their current position, afraid of the threat of redundancy, and usually increasing their own productivity to make themselves less disposable if and when the axe falls.

There is no hiding place. The competition for every job is going to be tough. Everyone is going to have to up their game.

After a period of years when the market was both job rich and candidate short, the tide has turned. Not only is it now job short and candidate rich, but those candidates are highly skilled, and employers are looking to reduce their risk by hiring staff who have precisely the skills and experience they need. Why wouldn't they? When there is a glut of good candidates, employers are spoilt for choice. There is absolutely no need for them to take unnecessary risks by taking chances on the people they hire.

I'd like to put a different spin on that picture of doom, gloom and negativity.

My positive take is this: rather than feeling too down, too depressed, too de-energized, **how could these shifts and changes in the market open up some new opportunities?**

Currently all businesses are trying to maximize their assets to secure a return. But there is one key asset that they seem determined to ignore. And that asset is people. To help cut operating costs businesses have been getting rid of staff, their most valuable asset. Now, as an entrepreneur, I see this as a great opportunity. What I say is that companies should be *in*vesting not *di*vesting. That logic will, I am convinced, start to take hold, and the pendulum will swing back again. The job market follows a classic cyclical pattern. It will take time. But it will happen.

Even though sectors like construction and architecture have taken a big hit, others are growing. As the population ages, the healthcare and domestic care sectors need more workers; the green energy market is expanding rapidly; the teaching profession is desperate for new recruits.

So, let's look at the state of the job market as an opportunity for *you*. If major corporates and large companies are letting quantities of staff go, then it will be the smaller, more flexible, more ambitious, more dynamic businesses that will have the nous to see this is a chance for them to attract the kind of high-class talent – and that means you – that they might not have been able to appeal to in the past.

Rather than joining a shaky, jittery corporate, why not get in now with a vibrant, fleet-footed company? These businesses are often working in innovative areas, because the little guys have to be more creative to compete. And they could be the corporate giants of tomorrow: remember that Virgin started off as a single record store, that Google was essentially an idea on the back of an envelope not much more than fifteen years ago.

What are the key qualities and skills employers are looking for?

Although this is a time for survival of the fittest, rather than concentrating on yourself and focusing on your own concerns and your needs – however tempting that is – try and think about what your potential employer is going to be looking for.

It is vital to get right inside their mind and understand what is driving them.

Here are three areas to think about which can help you answer an employer's current needs and reinvigorate a positive attitude.

1. Adding value

Time was when demonstrating application and commitment was the hot button: the key factor in landing a job – coming in early, working late has always been rated very highly by employers. But although that kind of diligent attitude is still a valuable attribute, it is no longer *the* critical factor.

Talking to company bosses, senior managers and recruitment companies, it is clear that from now on the number one question in the mind of anybody considering employing you will be (or it really *should* be): 'How much **value** can you bring to my company?'

Everybody is very cost-conscious, the economy is in decline, profits are down, businesses are not doing as well as they were doing before. There is no room for excess fat, for time-servers and time-wasters. So, when you are thinking about applying for a job and when you are preparing for an interview, ask yourself:

'Am I an asset or a liability?'

In this instance asset means you are adding value to a company, while liability means you add no value and therefore are just a cost.

That's the first of the questions I need you to ask yourself. You should be able to quantify any job or any role and demonstrate what it contributes to the firm. You are going to cost your employer a salary, National Insurance contributions, running costs. You, the employee, need to know what your cost is.

If you are on £30,000 a year, plus National Insurance of 12.8 per cent, that immediately puts you up to a basic cost of £33,840. On top of that you need to add in the cost of your desk and chair, the cost of your phone, your computer licences, your proportion of the rental rates, heating, lighting. All these ancillary costs caused by you sitting in an office are going to total a minimum of roughly £1,000 a month, and however you work the numbers out, the average is between £1,000 and £2,500 per month per person as an on-cost to salary.

So, whatever your salary is, you can add £12,000–£30,000 on top of the basic figure. And if you calculate the overall cost per year of your role in the company, will you be able to justify that cost? What can you do to prove that you are worth it? What can you do to make the person you want to hire you feel that, in the current market, this is a cost he or she is prepared to absorb?

And if you don't know the answer, then why don't you ask the question? Ask the employer the question. Imagine you are sitting in front of me, and at the end of the interview I ask you, 'Have you got any questions you'd like to ask?' You say: **'In this role, James, how could I make a contribution to your company?'**

What a great question.

Being able to quantify that contribution depends on the kind of job you want. In every job there is an output. It is a matter of determining what that output is. In every role there should be a direct measure. Every role can and should be able to be quantified, and you should be able to demonstrate that value.

In the most direct way, if you work in sales, you create and deliver revenue, which is easily measurable and very transparent, and because you have just won a new customer you can show that you are having a direct, measurable impact on the business. If you want a sales job and you can demonstrate to me that you are able to generate four times your income in sales value, that hiring decision is virtually a no-brainer.

In other roles, you have to find different measuring sticks. What are the criteria, the key performance indicators for your role? If you take the job of a PA, one absolutely critical measure is the amount of time a PA frees up for their boss. Whenever my PA is able to create an extra two or three hours a day for me, that is a great contribution to my company.

If you are going to an interview as a PA for a chief executive, as part of your preparation you can go to Companies House, where the chief executive's salary will usually be recorded, because generally he or she is the highest paid person in that business (and normally the highest paid person is listed in the accounts). There is absolutely no reason why a PA – why any future employee – should not search a Companies House listing.

If you see that the chief executive is earning x amount of money – be it £100,000, £200,000, half a million, whatever the figure is – he or she has their own on-cost as well, and that on-cost is naturally going to be greater than yours because they will have a larger office, all the support staff, a raft of expenses.

You can almost double the chief executive's salary. So, how can you – as a potential PA – justify your cost if you are hired?

All you have to do is demonstrate how you can make that chief executive more efficient, because every single minute of every day of a chief executive's time is extremely valuable. Every minute, every hour that you can save is *in*valuable.

If I was interviewing a PA and asked a candidate why I should hire them, the answer I would love to hear is: 'James, one of the reasons I think you should hire me is because my organization skills are immaculate. I am going to be totally focused on making sure that I can save you time. I can take away as much of the burden of administration as possible, supervise the planning, coordinate you better. I will make sure I get you to appointments on time, because I am going to check exactly how long it takes you to get to your appointment and precisely how long you need to be there.'

For example, twice a day my PA goes through all the emails I receive, creates a digest from them – the highlights of my emails – and prints that out for me. From that list, I can say, 'Let me have a look at this or that email.' Rather than reading a hundred, I may read only five. That alone saves me a good two hours a day. I believe that in every job you should be able to demonstrate how you add value. If in any capacity you can tell the employer how you save money, how you add value, that makes a big difference during a phase when everybody is very cost-conscious. This mood of cost-cutting is a change of mentality that will outlast the next upswing in the economy. Once companies get into the habit of being lean and mean, of creating and adopting efficiencies, the chances are they will stick to them.

And to be honest, proving that you add value to a company is valid whether there is a recession or not. Even when the market is doing a lot better, if you apply that methodology, it is never going to hold you back. It is always going to make you a more attractive candidate if you can show that you will be a 'high value for money' employee.

2. Using technology

The impact of technology is going to play an increasingly important role in the job market. Which job, which role in the business world, does not require the use of computer and IT skills?

Here is another area where you can demonstrate the specifics of what you are able to bring to a company. Define and quantify the use of technology in your particular role. Clearly some of us are better than others at manipulating and exploiting the power of technology. We are not all exactly the same, thank goodness. But how often do you think it emerges in an interview that you are an adept user of PowerPoint or Photoshop, or that you are experienced at modifying a website?

I learned the hard way to take advantage of new technology. When I was running the employment agency Alexander Mann, I employed two PAs. Whenever I walked into the office, my PC was already switched on, emails were printed out and placed on my desk. I scribbled on them and my PAs dealt with it. When I sold the business, I decided to set up an office at home, and went out and bought myself a computer. I was sitting there, wondering why this gleaming piece of kit didn't work. I rang one of my PAs and moaned, 'It's not working.' She said patiently, 'That's because you have to switch it on, James.' I switched it on. Nothing. 'Now you need a password.' It was that basic.

So, I forced myself to learn how to use a computer. I rang an agency and asked them to send me a temp PA. When she arrived I said, 'Actually, rather than you taking letters, could you just come round here and tell me what this icon means?' For a month she took me through everything. We did nothing else. She showed me how Photoshop worked, how download-ing worked. It was one of the most productive months I have ever spent, because even if all my PAs left, I could probably still do the job on my BlackBerry. If you are not computer-savvy, in my belief, you will not be able to function. The world has moved on. You can't live in the past.

We know that the employer is looking to justify the value of the employee. If you were sitting there in an interview and you asked me, 'James, does your company use this kind of technology, or have you ever considered using it, because I have found that it directly increased my team's efficiency?' you are demonstrating to me that not only do you have those specific technical skills, but – even better – you have spent time before the interview thinking about things that can make *my* company more effective, more efficient. Now, **how impressed do you think that is going to make me?**

One impact of technology on the job market is that there are more people working from home than ever before. Twenty

years ago, you had to go to an office, because all your information, all your files, the work you had done the day before had
to be stored there. Now, most people can work from home
without changing anything. I can log into my in-box from
home: all of a sudden all my emails, my folders and files are
available, and my screen is exactly the same as my screen at
work. So, there are a number of jobs you could apply for today
where you don't have to go into the office every day: another
reason to be as computer-savvy as possible.

3. Being realistic

While a period of economic turmoil does offer opportunities,
you should be realistic with your expectations. Take a good step
back, draw a deep breath and have a think about the long-term
impact of looking for a new job.

This book is not about career development – that's a whole
other book – and more than likely you have a clear idea of the
kind of job you really want.

But before you do anything else, I would like you to take
some time out to review the sector you are in or that you think
you would like to move into. Whether you are a school leaver, a
graduate, coming back into the workplace after a break raising
a family or following redundancy, or looking to change companies, you need to clarify, for yourself, that this move is the best
one for you – once you are clear in your mind about that, you
can approach the hassles and hurdles of the job search with a
positive mindset.

Although the vast bulk of advice in this book is applicable

to every job level and every job sector, there are, of course, differences between industries. As you review the landscape ahead, take into account those differences.

For example, if you are a lawyer, typically you will have a six-month notice period. How will that affect you getting a job? Because your long notice period creates a perception that you are not immediately available.

If you are just entering the job market, and plan to go into the media or fashion world, getting a job in that sector brings its own dynamic. If you want a first-time job with a magazine like *Vogue*, or as a sales assistant in a company like Louis Vuitton, you will start by earning very little money. If you are lucky, they might pay your expenses. They are able to pay you a low wage because they know that there is intense demand for those jobs and that there are far more people who want to work for that brand than there are jobs available. You could be an intern with them for a year and at the end of it not even get a job. You will have worked your socks off for no money because of the strength, the power, the appeal of the brand. Now, I am not against internships, but the reality is that there is never a guarantee of a full-time job.

If you are a graduate, feeling drawn to the glamour of a Louis Vuitton or a *Vogue*, you might imagine you would easily be able to earn big money, because the brand is successful, a household name – only to find that after putting in three years at university and coming out with a degree, the job pays no more than £10,000 a year. If you had known that before you started, would you still have done it?

My daughter studied at LSE, and of course a lot of her friends ended up in investment banking. That had been their specific objective in going to LSE. A year or so after graduating she told me that she had been talking to her friends and they were telling her how competitive, how aggressive it was, that the hours were gruelling because of global trading with one market opening as another closed, that there was huge pressure to perform and get results. She wondered how many of them had really thought about the reality – as opposed to the idea and the image – of going into that business.

Are you considering changing career?

I am frequently approached by people who do not know what career they should be in. These are not only graduates, but people who are already established in one particular business or profession – a lawyer, a banker, a fashion seller.

If you really feel trapped or demotivated in one sector, you should examine carefully the key drivers which are pushing you to consider swapping careers. Is it money; is it lifestyle; is it the content of the job; is it your fit within that new sector? As with all new job opportunities, I would like you to define what it is that you bring to the table, what makes you different from people who have been in that sector all of their career. Again, what value can you prove you will deliver to that new sector – and for yourself?

For *The Money Programme* on BBC2 I did a segment called 'James Caan's Jobs'. They wanted me to interview a range of candidates – there was a mechanical engineer based in Bolton, a banker from the City, a woman who worked for the travel side of American Express – and pick one of them to give some focused advice to. I chose Sherene, who worked for American Express. She'd been in their travel section for seven or eight years, and was now in her late twenties.

She told me, 'The problem I'm having is that the travel industry has changed enormously in the last ten years. Travel booking has become internet-based, and so the concept of the traditional travel agent doesn't really exist any more. But because that's what I have been doing for most of my adult life, I'm really struggling.'

I said, 'OK, let's look at the core skills that you have, your core competencies, and see whether we can transfer those skills into other sectors.' After talking to her, what stood out for me was that she had extremely strong customer service skills.

I happened to own a serviced-office company, and I knew that in that business her skills were really valuable. In the travel business a vital factor is building a relationship with the customer and providing a good service, rather like being a concierge in a hotel. And in a business centre offering serviced office space the requirement is quite similar. You go in, you can book offices, meeting rooms, video conferencing. You can have the office for a day, a week, a month. It's like a hotel for business – very much the same idea. It is equally important to build a good relationship, provide a good service, because the aim is to retain clients. And as it happened, at that time the serviced-office sector was performing really well as an industry, so recruiting good people was key.

I thought to myself, 'Sherene would be really good at this, because she has those interpersonal skills, she is smart, she's had a pretty solid job history, and the pay is quite similar, if not better.' When I suggested she apply to serviced-office companies, she had never thought about them – because she had never even heard of that kind of business. I suggested she look on the internet to find the top five players in the market, then rewrite her CV, placing her customer service skills right at the front. I advised her to make those skills very appropriate and relevant to the business centre environment, by spelling out that the reason she was applying for the position was that she understood the most important thing for those companies was the value of their clients, and retaining those customers. She worded her CV very well, sent it to five companies, got three interviews, and landed a job.

Sherene was delighted, of course. 'I can't believe it,' she said, 'I've been looking for a job for nine months, sending out CV after CV, getting nowhere. Now, after three weeks, I've got a job offer.'

The lesson was that sometimes it's about trying to understand not a job title but the actual component of the job. Talk to friends and people you know to explore which other industry sectors could value or benefit from your experience and skills.

There is constant evolution within different sectors. For example, for those employees over forty who are now working in IT, the opportunities in that industry simply didn't exist in any significant quantity when they were first starting out in the workplace after school or university. So, the systems maintainers and content managers might have initially had jobs as typesetters, filing clerks or teachers – but when the growth in IT offered a new opportunity, they grasped it with relish. Things move on. The cordwainers, scriveners and fletchers of yesteryear are the IT operatives of tomorrow.

Sometimes these desires for a career shift are surprising. I had an influx of letters from a number of lawyers and barristers asking for my advice on a career change. Even I couldn't have predicted that. I would instinctively have thought that certain areas of the legal sector were benefiting from the recession. Others are less surprising. There is a huge shortage in the teaching profession: many City workers decided to take the downturn as an opportunity to enter teaching. If you are uncertain about a future career path, a website like careerplayer.com, although designed for graduates, contains valuable information and advice for everybody, by using industry insiders to describe the pros and cons of a particular sector.

I am a great believer in people following their desires in business, but you really do need to pick the right time to give yourself the best chance of success. And to public sector workers I would pose these questions: should the issue of job security restrict your career? Or should you look for job progression in the private sector and potentially face a level of uncertainty?

The laws of economic supply and demand still apply. With more candidates looking for fewer jobs, the perceived 'price' of candidates will be driven down. It is quite possible that if you want to move to another company you will not be paid the salary that you would ideally want. You might take the view – as I tend to – that securing a smaller piece of something today is a better option than holding out for more and ending up with a big fat nothing.

Is there an impact because of gender or age?

My personal experience has been that, all things being equal, I prefer to hire women. I find that women are generally more loyal and hard-working, and that women in executive positions tend to be more driven than men because there are fewer of them, they have to work smarter, and they have to perform and deliver because they know that's the only way that they will get noticed.

Whenever I am recruiting for a management or executive position, and I have a selection of candidates, if there is a woman in the batch of candidates, her CV is always going to be noticed by me, because I have had good experiences hiring women. It is the same if you have ever hired anyone from a particular company who has worked out well – mentally you will have a natural bias towards any applicant coming from the same company because you assume that company tends to hire good people.

One of the best investments I ever made was a business called Alexander Mann Solutions, started by Rosaleen Blair, who went on to build the most successful business I've invested in. My first investment in *Dragons' Den* was with a woman, Sammy French, and her Fit Fur Life dog treadmill. From a gender perspective my experience has always been that I've been more successful with women in employment than otherwise.

I know that goes against the norm. Women tell me they often think that they are not as good, that there is still a glass ceiling, and that the jobs they really want don't exist. I don't accept that. I think there are opportunities. Clearly there is competition. And there are not as many opportunities or organizations that prefer women. Men obviously do well. There are a lot of them, they hog the senior management positions, they dominate the boards of FTSE 100 companies. But I expect to see that balance change over the next ten to fifteen years.

One school of thought considers that if more women had held senior positions in banking and finance, the collapse of the financial markets in 2008–2009 might have been much less severe, if not averted – and that women will be instrumental in helping the UK recover from recession.

Merit alone should be the determining factor in getting a job, and discrimination law is designed to rectify any imbalance, though it will take time to root it out – how many women applying for senior management positions are still asked if they have children or if they are planning to? Ageism remains a continuing challenge for recruitment consultants and candidates alike – the 2006 Age Discrimination Act is making an impact, and now dates of birth must be excluded from any CV. However, the reality is that simply removing your date of birth is fine, but if you have thirty or forty years of work experience, it is a simple matter for an employer to deduce the age of an applicant.

To counter that, read every job description very carefully and look for areas of your expertise that are an appropriate match. With age comes experience, and that is a valuable commodity.

If you are about to graduate, what should you be bearing in mind?

This is particularly relevant in a period when there are more students graduating every year than ever before, and there is a decrease in job opportunities.

The graduate job market is tough, because not only are the corporates and blue-chip companies cutting their graduate schemes – the traditional 'milk round' – but graduates represent a batch of people who have, essentially, the same qualification. I am not sure that employers differentiate between a 2.1 and a first. In other words the degree or grade you have doesn't really count. The qualification is good to have, but it is not a decision maker.

So, how do you stand out? This is the point at which personality kicks in as an absolute must. As a graduate you are not selling your CV, you are selling yourself, who you are, what your values are, your beliefs, your drives, your motivations.

From what I have observed and experienced, I would say that very few graduates have actually sat down and thought about the questions every job candidate should ask: **What are my characteristics? What are my USPs? What are the features and benefits I can offer to an employer?**

Graduates often waste too much of their time trying to craft their CV. They go back to their Duke of Edinburgh's Awards or their time as head boy or head girl. That is all interesting material, but rarely compelling: it doesn't exactly lift off the page. As an employer what I am really interested in is, 'Who are you? What do you stand for? What do you bring to the table?' When I am interviewing a graduate, these are, for me, the decision-making issues. I'd almost like to see a graduate CV dealing only with answers to those questions.

But I have found over the years, a graduate can fill three pages with details of their dissertation, yet include nothing about any practical experience, whether they have the discipline to turn up for work every day, whether they can take on responsibility, whether they are prepared to knuckle down to a task.

I was giving a talk at Cambridge University. There were 300 people in the room and I am sure many of them were sitting there as graduates thinking, 'I'd love to work for someone like James Caan.' Yet only a handful waited until the conference was finished and approached me directly. They were the few who had the confidence and the initiative to make a difference.

One of them was a young woman called Abby, who said, 'I would really like to come and see you. This is what I've done.' She gave me what we call the 'elevator pitch', those few minutes travelling up in the lift when you can make an impression. And what did I do? I bought the determination she showed in her eyes, the passion, the drive.

Abby came into the Hamilton Bradshaw offices and I introduced her to three or four of the managers. And now she looks after our *Dragons' Den* investments. Every time I invest in somebody from the Den she takes care of that entrepreneur, provides them with any support they need, makes sure that they have got a viable business plan. But the fact she had gone to Cambridge would not have swung the job for her, because if she had not performed well at the interview, having a degree from Cambridge would not have saved it for her.

Employment is far too competitive to assume that just because you went to a certain university you are going to get a job. I don't believe that any more. Being hired as a graduate is no different from being hired later in your career. You still have to perform, you still have to deliver. You still have to show a positive enthusiasm for the job you want.

Are you coming back to the workplace after a period away?

The harsh truth is that you will always be a much more attractive candidate if you are in a job than if you are not in a job. Just as we always want to go to the club that we're not a member of – it is the same principle. When you are already working, psychologically you are in a position of strength because you do not *have* to take the new job. And that means the interviewer has to work a bit harder. If you are not in a job, the interviewer knows that you need a job, which gives them the upper hand. If you have the choice, always apply while you are still working.

However, if you have been made redundant or are returning to work after a period raising a family, or following an illness, you don't have that choice. You need to stay positive.

A redundancy in particular is a huge shock to the system. You need to recover, regroup, make sure you structure your job search, and really think about the skills you have gained from your previous experience. Write down your key skills and think about how they could be applied in other sectors.

Transferable skills in isolation are not enough to secure a career in a different industry. A few years ago the 'golden' set of skills that you hear recruiters and employers talking about might well have provided a stepping stone into a new industry. But not any more. The recession means the job market is saturated with skilled candidates. In a recession recruiters will push the safe set of buttons.

If you are returning to work after some years away, take time to adjust to the changes that have happened in the meantime: the impact of technology, the change in presentation – no more power dressing.

But, as always, be realistic. The team at webrecruit, an online recruitment company I invested in, have noticed a trend for overqualified candidates to apply for any role, regardless of salary, to secure work. They tell me it's commonplace to hear from senior-level candidates who are frustrated because they are not getting any interviews.

Don't view being overqualified as a negative, inhibiting factor. I imagine you will have spent much of your working life developing skills, so finding a role that suits your aspirations is the common-sense thing to do. From an employer's perspective, they're probably worried that if they ask you to take on a job at an apparently lower level, you might leave in a few months' time for a role better suited to your career aspirations.

Consider other options. Flexibility in the workplace is an advantage. If you have senior management experience, there is a demand for experienced interim managers, brought into a company for a fixed period to see it through a specific short-term problem, a re-structuring or nursing a company through the recession.

If you are searching for part-time work, have you considered registering with a temping agency? Less obviously: consider home-based, commission-only roles. If you're already out of work – what's the risk?

I recently became involved with **v**, a national young volunteers service. Working with them has cemented my belief that including volunteering on your CV will improve your employability. It is an ideal way to showcase your skills, and help secure work, particularly if you're young and have limited commercial experience. The act of volunteering has undergone a radical change in style: there is a vast range of rewarding projects that can open up a wealth of opportunities, fit round your existing commitments *and* develop your CV.

And above all, improving your skills – through online courses or adult education – will vastly increase your value to an employer. Whenever I see on a CV that someone has used a period of time off to develop their abilities and capabilities, I take that as a huge positive, an indication that they have remained committed and motivated even when things are not going so well – just what I want to see in my staff.

How committed are you to getting a new job?

Are you looking for a move because it offers more money? Are you looking because you want to take on more responsibility? Or are you looking because there has been a recent promotion at work which you thought you were going to get, but found yourself pipped at the post? In other words: are you just fishing for fun?

I would be looking to change companies every three or four

years, because that offers the fastest route to accelerate your career, since every move will generally represent a shift up in status, responsibility and salary. If you do not move, that does not mean you're not succeeding, but the pace of your progression is going to be slowed down because of it.

On your own – outside any scheduled internal appraisals – you should always think about your job every twelve months, reviewing the progress you have made, a kind of annual career MOT. Every year set yourself a goal for the coming year: taking on a new responsibility, mastering a new skill. In any task or any function one year is long enough to demonstrate whether you can or cannot add value. At the end of each year intellectually you are ready to take the next step. You don't leap from being a sales manager to an MD, or from a PA to the head of HR. But you set yourself very clear goals for the end of each twelve months to go to the next level up, one step at a time, and you keep notching your way forward.

Ask your line manager, 'What can I do, what do I need to demonstrate, to progress in this company?' People admire employees who add value to the organization. Always ask yourself, **'If somebody was measuring my contribution, what would my scorecard look like?'**

'Do I make a difference within this company? Do I add value by what I do?' If the answer is no, it is pretty obvious that your career development in the company will be significantly hampered.

If you have asked yourself all these questions, setting the framework for your decision to go for another job, and at the end of that process you feel that perhaps you have not been making the most of the opportunities available in your current company, you could make a brave decision to stay and really work those opportunities. Take on more responsibility, learn more skills, make your ambition known, put yourself on the radar.

Perhaps the best piece of advice you will take from this book is that the job you really need right now is the job you are in, but the difference is that you are going to transform its potential.

And if you have asked yourself all these questions, and you are still determined to move, great. That is a positive, informed, considered decision. Now you can make the time and the space to give yourself the very best chance.

I need you to be 100 per cent committed to this next job move, because it could be the job that transforms your career, transforms your life and your lifestyle. I need you to be ready to put in the hard work, the preparation, the attention to detail that will improve your chances tenfold. **Are you ready? Let's go.**

"I am always looking for a glimpse, a glint of real passion for a job. It's a clue for me that you have the mix of enthusiasm and conviction that leads to success."

2. PASSION

I strongly believe that if you take charge of your own destiny *and* have a real desire, a genuine passion, for the job you want, this will prove an unbeatable combination.

When the job market is tougher and keener than ever before, and the number of applicants for a job often frankly astonishing, passion is an essential component of your job-hunting kit. And one of the best ways to demonstrate that passion is to get out there and be proactive. It is no good sitting back and hoping that the job you really want will magically come to you, or leaving everything up to recruitment agencies and consultants. You need to roll up your sleeves and put in the effort yourself. I was told by one candidate recently that she was convinced that the 'hidden' job market – those positions filled under the radar, not through agencies, adverts or job boards – was seventy per cent of the total. I disagreed, and told her, 'Those jobs are not hidden. You're just not looking in the right place.'

How can you be proactive in sourcing a job?

As you start your search for the job you really want, you should follow a classic business maxim: find a need and fill it. On one episode of *Dragons' Den* Peter Moule, who was running his family's electrical engineering business, pitched us a product called the Chocbox, which in essence made connecting electrical cables a doddle. There was an immediate bidding war because we all saw that electricians needed this product to save them fretting over health and safety regulations. The Chocbox filled the need. As soon as that became obvious, it was a question of *who* would end up giving Peter the investment, not *if* anybody would.

When you are looking for a job, the same principle applies. Channel your efforts by targeting those companies that are going to want to give you a job. Fill their need. Winning an interview is all about sending your CV to a company that fits you and which you fit too. Let's cut out anything which feeds negativity. Getting that interview will give you all the positive energy you need.

Finding the right company with the right job for you

The job market is more fluid than it has ever been. Statistically more people change jobs and companies than they have ever done before – it's what's called 'churn' in the business. This is partly due to the volatility caused by the recession, but it also reflects the fact that people have recognized that when they move to a new company they will typically move up in responsibility and status and will get paid more.

Volatility provides opportunities: and your decision is whether a) you use professional help, from recruitment agencies and headhunters, to find your way through all the options, b) you apply direct to companies, or c) you make yourself prominent, visible and marketable in the digital marketplace.

My question to you is: **Why not do all three, and exploit every route available?**

Your sole aim is to reach the person, the decision maker, who is going to offer you the right job. In order to achieve that, use all the options out there. The secret is to use them wisely.

There is no point in adopting a scattergun approach. Don't 'spray and pray'. That will simply be a waste of your precious time and energies.

Building a relationship with agencies

How many headhunting and recruitment firms exist today compared to ten or twenty years ago? I suspect the figure has tripled. That proliferation reflects the fact that more people are moving around, because recruitment agencies are targeting people in a fast-moving, fluid environment. HR departments within companies – understaffed and overloaded – need the help of agencies and headhunters to source the best people available for the job on offer at any given time.

As far as agencies are concerned, the key word for me is 'specialist'. In the job market today, the recruitment industry has become highly specialized. Thirty years ago it was a generalist industry covering every area. Since then it has become incredibly focused and highly specialist – eighty per cent of agencies specialize in specific sectors, and even the large, broad-based agencies like Michael Page or Reed have a string of specialist divisions. If you are an upfield oil and gas worker, there's an agency just for you. If you are an actuary, you will find a specialist in your discipline.

Why as an employer would I use an agency? If I run a chain of shops and I am looking for a store manager, I am more likely to go to a headhunting firm to find that person because I have a very specific need: I want somebody who knows how to run a store of a certain size, and with those criteria, an agency will be able to target candidates equally specifically. Clearly, somebody who is already successful in that particular function is far more valuable than somebody without that relevant experience.

If I wanted to go and look for that store manager myself, it could take six months of searching. As an employer I will be weighing up six months' investment of time and cost versus paying an agency a fee to provide somebody who could walk through the door today. That obviously carries a premium for the employer. When companies are under pressure just to survive, offloading to an agency all the work required to source a good candidate, even with the fee involved, may well be much more cost-effective.

As a candidate, there is a lot you can do proactively to make an agency's life easier. With more and more applicants, their problem is how to pick the right candidate from so many options. So, make their life easier by building a relationship with specific consultants who can then become your personal champion.

The key is finding the right consultant who has the contacts and the relationships with those companies that will have the kind of job you want. And by the right consultant, I mean a particular person within the agency. This is where you can be proactive in sourcing who that person is. Look on the agency's website at the consultant team, and find who matches your sector best. Talk to friends and colleagues who have used agencies to get similar jobs, and find out which consultants were most successful in reaching the right decision maker.

You can also ask them to tell you which posts they have successfully filled in your area in the last year. Tony Seager, an experienced recruitment consultant and trainer I work with, told me he had a CEO of a software services company come to see him, and he quizzed Tony on his credentials as a recruiter, very specifically on how many jobs at that level he had filled. Candidates asking for credentials, or getting testimonials from other clients, used to be commonplace in the recruitment business, but that is rare now. That does not mean you can't do that to satisfy yourself that you are working with the right person, the right team, the right agency.

This is a two-way relationship. Don't think of a recruitment consultant as simply a middleman. A good consultant will be able to give you expert advice on careers, on specific jobs, coach you for the interview – and all for free! The cost is going to be borne by the employer. Successful agencies are keen to move away from simplistic matching processes, and want to get under the skin of potential candidates, to find out what their individual motivations and ambitions are – their key 'drivers' to use industry jargon. You can help a consultant by, for example, giving them a list of companies you would work for, and those you would not – on whatever grounds are relevant – to help steer them on your behalf.

Since I own two agencies which specialize in public sector jobs – Attenti Executive Recruitment, which focuses on senior-level appointments for local government, charities and the NHS, and Matrix, which operates across the board for public authority jobs – there is a general point I would like to make about the difference between the public and private sectors in terms of getting a job.

In fact the point I really want to make is that as far as the ideas and advice in this book are concerned, there is not that much of a difference. My knowledge of the public sector leads me to believe that everything I am talking about is just as appropriate and that you should not compromise on any of these ideas simply because of the processes involved in finding jobs in the public sector.

Yes, the method of recruitment might be a bit more bureau-cratic, the forms lengthier, the protocol more rigid. But ultimately you still have to turn up for an interview, you still have to perform at that interview, you still have to demonstrate your ability to communicate. There may also be less leeway involved in negotiating the ultimate package, as the salary bands tend to be quite narrow and specific, but in every other aspect I think you will find that the thrust and attitude of this book is completely relevant.

Plunging into the digital talent pool

Alongside your review of the agency market, get out and get noticed. Adapt yourself to the current climate. Explore every opportunity that new technology offers. The World Wide Web has had a huge impact on the job market, just like every other aspect of work. As part of my portfolio of companies I have invested in online recruitment companies alongside traditional and specialist companies.

Thanks to the internet and digital technology, you can easily, almost instantaneously, become part of the talent pool. I recommend using online job boards. Recruiters trawl CV databases on a daily basis, looking to match candidates to jobs. Now employers are also using them directly.

In the space of only a few years, job boards have grown to represent the largest single market. More candidates are sourced through job boards than via any other means. And the key for you is that they have evolved to mirror the specialization of both traditional press ads and recruitment agencies. There are niche job boards for secretarial positions, job boards for accounting, job boards for doctors – you name it. The internet is at its best whenever there are precise search criteria involved: specialist boards will make the right connections efficiently and rapidly.

Of course there are general job boards which cover all sectors and areas. I would never exclude those general boards – since you should consider *every* potential route to the right job, and rule out none – but the reality is that you are more likely to succeed by using a specialist board, because typically that is what your key employer group is going to be targeting. I have heard the general job boards described as 'cattle markets', compared to the 'quality farmers' markets' of the specialist job boards. There are tools out there to help you select the most effective job boards for your needs: websites which track applicant responses to ads and highlight the most effective boards.

A word of warning: look around a job board first and get a feel for the kind of jobs advertised, and just as with agencies, talk to friends and colleagues who may have used the board to see how effective they found it. Posting your CV on a board or a database is quick and easy, but it can go viral in a mouse-click. You are no longer in control of who can see it. Or it may simply disappear into a cyberspace loop and never be looked at by anyone again. The net offers quantity but not always quality.

And of course you can use the internet yourself to target companies. If you happen to be, for the sake of argument, working in FMCG, go on to Google and key in, 'What are the top twenty FMCG companies in the UK?' You will find that somebody, somewhere will have compiled a league table for a newspaper or magazine and those top twenty names will come up.

Once you have found the names of those companies, head to their individual company websites, where you will, more often than not, find a Careers section. These corporate career pages are now a standard element of major company websites: all the jobs within companies such as Marks and Spencer, Shell or Unilever, will be listed, but increasingly the same is true of mid-sized and smaller companies. Don't look once. Make a note to return on a regular basis to the pages for companies you have targeted.

With the information gleaned from the site you can go direct to the employer, and post your CV on to their job board. At Hamilton Bradshaw we have a Careers section on our site, and I would say that fifty per cent of the people we hire have come directly from our own website. I know that figure is slightly skewed because I have become something of a brand name, which brings a higher level of traffic to the Hamilton Bradshaw site. But the principle is the same, and an indication of how things will continue to evolve.

The beauty of the internet is also that it is global, it transcends frontiers. So, if you want a job in America, and you are looking for recruitment agencies in the States that specialize in your sector, or the top ten employers in Chicago, or job boards which specialize in your particular sector, you can find them on the net.

Take advantage of the networks that exist online. Add yourself to a business and professional listing like LinkedIn or set yourself up on Twitter. You can join recruitment discussions via social networking sites. There are websites aimed at bringing soon-to-be graduates into contact with major brands. The opportunities for sourcing job openings proliferate monthly. There are job sections within general classified ad sites. Jobs are increasingly being advertised as bite-sized tweets with a link you can follow up for more information. Online companies you already have a link with are sending email shots listing career opportunities.

Here's a second word of warning: there is so much information available, that you could easily spend all day every day online, and be swamped. The Web can at its best help you find a needle in the haystack – but it's a hell of a big haystack . . . Keep yourself focused and targeted.

And there is another great network you should exploit – not digital, but human: your own contacts. Recruitment agents regularly map out candidates' contacts, but you are best placed to do that yourself. Who do you know as a client, supplier, competitor who might be the link to your next job?

Not least – and as somebody who owns recruitment companies, I shouldn't really be saying this – direct contact by a potential employee, which means the saving of a recruitment fee, will be attractive to many employers.

In the current climate I am not sure there is great value in simply approaching companies on the off-chance and asking to be kept on file in case a suitable job comes up in the future. It is too hit and miss, not targeted enough. It might yield results, but not in the immediate term, so if you want a job now it probably is not going to be that valuable. But if you have a specific reason for a speculative approach – maybe you have read about a company moving into a new product area in which you have direct experience – then you will be offering real value.

Those of us who have been working for years have had to adjust to the impact of technology – but if you are just entering the job market, you will not necessarily know that the role job boards fulfil used to be filled by press ads. There are still plenty of ads in newspapers, both local and national, with the major broadsheets carrying adverts for specific industries and sectors on a weekly basis. Check the newspapers and the trade press just as much as the online boards.

I think of all these routes as a funnel channelling you to a specific job. In the end you have to come down to a job that you fit and which fits your needs. Otherwise you are just wasting your time.

The JC twist

If you read about a job you think might have been right for you, but it has already been filled, why not contact that company in three to four months' time? You might just find that the candidate they chose has not worked out during the trial period – it happens more than you might think – and just when the line manager is at their wit's end, you could appear like a white knight on the horizon.

Raising your own profile

You can be proactive in getting yourself known throughout your industry sector. This is particularly relevant in certain careers – media, PR and journalism, for example – where your reputation is a critical element of your value as a 'commodity available for hire', where you will be rated in terms of your link to certain articles you have written, clients you have worked with – so, whoever happens to be George Clooney's or Angelina Jolie's agent will always be branded as that in people's minds. It is an association that adds value, that becomes a real currency.

But equally in other industries you can increase that perception of your value by making yourself visible outside the cocoon of your own company – attending conferences, dinners, writing in the trade press, blogging. You may not always feel like going out to another trade dinner, but remember that it might just be that dinner where you make a contact with somebody who will later offer you a fantastic job. You are making an investment to enhance the value of your personal brand.

I came across a great example of this when I was in America, looking to buy a particular recruitment company. I was spending a week touring a number of their offices and the directors kept mentioning one consultant, Cindy, who was their top biller, by a mile – she was billing over five times the average amount. I was intrigued to learn more about her success, and on the fourth or fifth day I finally got to meet her.

'Cindy,' I asked her, 'tell me a bit about what you do: what's the market you're in?'

'Windows, James, that's what I do.'

I immediately thought she must specialize in software programmers, of course.

'No,' she said, 'I mean those square things in buildings.'

I couldn't believe that was an area of recruitment big enough to make her the star biller – I would have thought she was in investment banking, or law, or FMCG.

Absolutely not. She placed people in the window business. And because Cindy was the biggest brand name in that sector, everybody came to her. That was why she billed so much every year.

She told me that she had started out recruiting in the construction area, but she realized there were too many other consultants in that field. She needed to carve out a niche. So, she settled on the window business, took courses, visited every industry event, went to every product launch, got to know the suppliers, the fitters, architects, engineers. Cindy ended up knowing so much about the business, and so many people within it, that many clients retained her on an annual basis simply for her knowledge. If there was a takeover or an acquisition, she knew the personnel, the ins and outs of every organization.

The lesson of this story, from a career perspective, is that Cindy had understood the value of her personal brand, and the difference between being good and being great. In most industries the price differential between being good and being great is fifty per cent. If you are competent at your job, you might be on £50,000, for example. If you are great at that job, and you make sure people recognize that, you could be on £75,000.

The JC twist

Let's say I am your employer, and you are high-profile in the industry. I am not stupid: I can see that your profile means that you are visible to my competitors. And therefore I am probably going to have to recognize that you are being approached. I will have to be on my toes to make sure your remuneration is in line with the market. Because if I'm not, I won't be your employer for long. You will move on. So, your high profile effectively puts the employer on notice.

Matching yourself to employers' needs

Be proactive too in understanding a potential employer's needs. Read between the lines of any job advert. If you see an ad saying: 'Go-getter salesperson needed', that seems obvious at first glance, but think about what the employer is really telling you.

The message here is, 'I need a sales person who is highly motivated, can operate independently, and can sell in large quantities.' Straight away you have three areas to focus on, allowing you to craft your experience to those needs, coming up with examples of how you have delivered precisely those things in your current and any previous jobs. If you can prove you are motivated, independent and a good seller, that employer is going to say, 'I need this person on my team.'

Here's an idea to bear in mind which allows you to prove that in a very direct – and challenging – way.

I was really impressed when one candidate said to me, 'James, I don't know about you, but I've always found that with interviews, it is quite difficult to work out whether this is the right opportunity for me and whether from your perspective I can really make a difference to this organization.'

He went on to say, 'What I wanted to propose was this: how would you feel about me coming in and spending a week here actually doing the job – at no cost to you, entirely at my own cost – to demonstrate to you that I can really make a difference? And most importantly to prove that I can add value to the position that you are offering?'

That was a fantastic question. If we had been playing a game of tennis, that would have been a point in his favour, possibly as important as a set point. If I said yes to him, then among all the other candidates the job was his to lose, because he would have every opportunity to go way beyond the interview process and actually do the job for a week. And even if I said no, it had told me a lot about him – that he had confidence and enough passion to take the risk of giving up a week of his own time for nothing.

From your point of view, as a potential employee, why wouldn't you ask the question?

This is central to my message. **The skill lies in the questions, never in the answers.**

The ability to ask these kinds of questions puts you streets ahead of your competition. And how many people do you think would have the confidence and the foresight to ask that question? I can tell you: very, very few.

When that candidate asked me whether he could come and work with us for a week, I had to take a deep breath. His question completely threw me. I thought to myself, 'I can't really say no,' but on the other hand I had not previously considered the question and so had not thought about the logistics and the implications. Yet I was also seriously impressed, precisely because the candidate had put me in a tight position. What did I do? I said, 'That's really interesting. Let me give that some thought and see what I can do.' I managed to avoid having to commit there and then, and gave myself some space to reflect on the question. Fifteen all!

By the way, you can equally apply this approach to the

company you are working in now. I had a situation recently where somebody in one of my businesses approached me and said, 'Could I come and see you, because I'd like to have a mentor within the organization?' I met with him and he said, 'I'm really happy in the company, and I feel that things are going really well. But I'm looking ahead over the next three years and beyond. What I want to know from you, James, is this: which areas do you think I need to improve on in order to be recommended at the next promotion?'

Again, I thought that was a great question. We spent some time discussing the areas he could improve and focus on. One of the things we agreed was that I would allow him to be an observer of the managers in other departments and functions. His motivation was that he was a sales director at the time, but if he was ever going to become managing director he would need to understand how all the other functions and departments worked. He felt that he was always going to get overlooked because he would seem one-dimensional. 'In order for me to have greater breadth,' he said, 'I want to understand how the HR department works, how the finance department works, and what their key issues are. It's not that as management I am going to have to do that, but I think I ought to know.' I thought that was smart.

When people tell me, 'I'm up for promotion and I'm going to wait for something to happen,' I wonder if that is the best strategy. The message here is that you can be far more proactive by asking yourself what you are achieving, and where you want to be.

If there is someone within your organization who has a role you believe that you would love to be in, why not approach that person and ask them to be your mentor? If you feel you want to be in a different department but you don't have the experience – which is inevitably what the company will say – why not approach the company? Tell them, 'I'm really happy where I am. I'm really enjoying it, but from a career perspective I'd like to get to know the organization better. I'd like to understand how some of the other functions in the departments work. I know that Marketing has a meeting once a month, to discuss strategy. Is it possible for me to join one of those meetings as an observer?'

The word 'observer' is very unthreatening. But taking that step immediately puts you on the radar of management. Your proactive initiative tells them, 'Here is somebody who has put their hand up.' People rarely do this. What they tend to say is, 'I've been here for four years and I've not been promoted. There are no career prospects.'

Well, career prospects don't just happen. Career prospects are what you create. It's all down to you. When people do well, they don't do well just because the company's doing well. When you are doing well, it's about your achievements, it's about what you want. I don't think enough people understand that.

Companies are built by people: people make a difference, people make a contribution. **Are you going to be part of the crowd or are you the somebody who stands out in the crowd?**

When you have amassed all your research, whether that's from the internet, the trade press or talking to friends in the business, and you feel you have the information you need to make a decision about the kind of job and the kind of company you are going to target, take one day out – go fishing, play a few sets of tennis or a round of golf, visit a museum, have an afternoon of retail therapy – whatever is your favourite way of relaxing. Getting away from the work environment will give you a sense of perspective. After all, this is your future you're about to change.

Bringing passion into play

I have said that demonstrating passion is a vital part of this process. Passion will sell you. But there is a balance needed in terms of thinking about how to convey your passion for a new job. Try to avoid being passionate about anything that will bring a negative attitude to the process.

For example, if the primary reason you want to find a job is for money, however strongly that might be your personal motivating factor, for me that is a weak point. The only reason a weak point can become a significant point is if there is a fundamental reason behind that decision.

If your pitch to an employer is going to be, 'I'm currently

earning £40,000 a year, but I'm getting married at the end of the year and we're thinking of moving into a new house, so money is really important to me now because I'm trying to build a future for myself and my partner,' that is a perfectly acceptable position. You are saying that up until now money had not really been a significant issue, but an event has happened to make it more important. Maybe you have now got young children and would like to send them to private school. Again that provides a specific reason for wanting a higher salary: 'I'm now at a stage in my life where I want to be in an environment where I can progress financially as well as from a career perspective.'

As an employer I actually respect that. Because what that really tells me is that you are driven, that you have a goal, that you are prepared to work hard, that you are prepared to make sacrifices because there is an event in your life that is very important to you.

If money *is* the issue you need to be ready to communicate that desire in a manner that makes it sound balanced, plausible and reasonable, rather than just saying, 'I'm on £36,000 a year now, and I'm applying because this job offers £45,000.' That comment would put me off, because what I will immediately be thinking is that if you are prepared to leave your last employer because somebody has offered you a bit more money, then it is highly likely that should you come to my company, if somebody else offers you a bit more money twelve months later, you are probably going to move again. And with that in my mind the chances are that I am not going to select you.

Conversely you need to be careful about showing too strong, too passionate a dislike for your previous employer. One of the earliest questions you are going to get in the process is, **'Why are you leaving?' At that point I would say as many as thirty per cent, even forty per cent of candidates fail because of their response to that single question.**

However you respond to that question the potential employer is thinking, 'How are you going to feel about *our* organization?' If your reply to the question is, 'I am leaving because there are no career prospects,' my immediate reaction is, 'Well, actually I need to know whether you can do the job you are applying for with my company, before I even contemplate the next stage.' Saying that there are no career prospects in your previous company is not a great response.

People seem to feel a need, because they're leaving an existing job, to justify the act of departure, and they think the way to do that is to reinforce the decision with a raft of negatives. I don't think that's a smart thing to do at all.

Saying anything negative about your existing employer is generally not going to be a mark in your favour. Treating the recruitment process as therapy for your personal woes, sitting there moaning about your previous company, doesn't help me one bit, and in my analysis more often than not it will go against you.

You know you are going to be asked the question about why you want to leave your current employer. It's not a trick question, and it is never a surprise. So, you should be fully primed and ready with your answer: 'It's a great company. I've really enjoyed working there, my colleagues have included some very good people. But I just feel right now that I'm at a position where I've learned as much as I can. I've climbed as high as I think I can in that particular organization. I've had a number of conversations with my line manager and – regrettably – there isn't any other opportunity to enhance my career. Otherwise I'd be really happy.'

That is a big tick in the box for me. I know that the position you're applying for is at a higher position than you have currently, which is why you're applying, and I accept that. I can hear that you have enjoyed working at the other company, that you have learned a lot, that you've been well looked after. For me that's perfectly acceptable. I can imagine you showing the same passion, and having the same positive attitude about my own company, if and when you decide to move on. And that makes me feel good about you.

When you're interviewing somebody who's already in a job, as an interviewer one of the first things you want to establish is whether a candidate is merely window-shopping or is genuinely committed to leaving.

If your answer to the question about leaving a company is too vague, that also sends out the wrong signal. It tells me you are simply fishing around. It's like being a house owner: every now and then you want to get your house revalued, just to see what the state of the market is, even though in your heart you are not the least bit committed to selling. There are people who apply for jobs because they are curious to see what the possibilities are, but who have no serious intention of changing companies.

As an experienced interviewer I would pick that up. Because when I ask that question, 'What is it about the existing company that you're not happy with, and why are you considering leaving?' if your response is very woolly, if I can't see the logic, it is pretty obvious to me that your interest is superficial. And if there is not enough differential between the package you are on at the moment and the package on offer, I know instinctively you're probably not going to take the job.

Again, you are looking for ways to communicate a passionate desire, rather than a *dis*passionate desire. But if you have been made redundant, and are feeling under pressure to get a job, any job, you need to convert that rather fraught passion into something more positive.

In those circumstances you should try hard not to come across as desperate. If you say to me, in a very diplomatic way, that you have four other opportunities you are exploring, or that you have met a couple of other organizations that you have been really impressed with, that puts you back into the position of saying, 'I'm in demand.'

The power of passion

My mantra has always been: 'Observe the masses, and do the opposite.' So, if you a) source the job you want, and b) match the needs of that employer to your experience, I believe that you will have dramatically improved your chances of getting that job. However, there are exceptions to the rule. Sometimes the passion and the grit are enough.

There is a guy who works for me called Will. When he applied to Hamilton Bradshaw he wanted to move into private equity. Normally to get a job in private equity you need to have a background as an investment banker, or a lawyer, or an accountant – and to have been a good one at that.

Will is not an accountant, not a lawyer, not really a banker, but he *is* a very strong marketeer. Private equity firms do not usually hire marketeers because the investment managers themselves go out and originate the deals. Yet when you look at the characteristics of an investment manager, the very fact that they are by training an accountant, a lawyer or a banker means it is unlikely they will be a good originator. The characteristics are conflicting.

I met Will, and initially was looking for reasons to turn him down because he lacked the 'relevant' experience. But after talking to him, I went completely out on a limb and offered him the job. I am sure no other private equity firm would have hired him because on paper he was completely wrong for the job, or at least for the received perception of the job. But what I saw at the interview was Will's passion.

I told him, 'Private equity is about investment and capital and returns. You haven't worked for an accounting firm, you haven't worked in a bank, and you've never run a business. Why would I hire you?'

But he wouldn't give up. He kept clutching at every piece of experience he could find, but in doing that, I saw something in him. I thought that if he was in front of a potential client he could convince them that Hamilton Bradshaw would be the right partner for them. He had plenty of passion, and bags of belief.

I went against convention. I thought, 'We already have good lawyers, accountants and bankers working for us. The things Will lacks, we have as strengths. But the component he has – those marketeer's skills – we don't have. He has presence, he has charm. When he walks into a room, he connects. An accountant doesn't necessarily connect when he walks into a room. All the bits that Will would struggle with, we have people working here who can do them. If I could give him access to draw those people in when he needs them, he could be quite good.'

I spoke to a couple of the guys internally and they were quite cynical. They said, 'James, we're not a sales organization. We don't sell. Private equity is quite a sophisticated financial business.' They all thought I'd lost it a bit.

But my view was that, ultimately, lawyers and accountants and bankers only come into play when there is a deal. What happens if there's no deal? What happens if we don't find a deal? Because finding the deal is just as important as negotiating it correctly. It's like winning the lottery: you've got to buy the ticket first. If there's no ticket, you're never going to win.

I decided to give it a shot and we took him on. And guess what? He is the most prolific originator in the firm. He has brought in more business than anyone else.

As a result we have adapted our model of what an investment manager is. What we realized was that when you have a function that's not working, maybe that is because you are expecting too much from one human being. When you actually break a job down, you realize there are components or characteristics in that role which you are not going to get from one individual. One human being cannot possess all of those attributes.

Essentially we used to have a model of an investment manager that was the same as everybody else's: he goes out, finds a deal, originates the deal, does the due diligence, handles the commercials, the negotiations, closes the deal, and then sits on the board. We have broken that job into four roles now. We don't believe that one person is ever going to be good at every one of those components. By going against the grain, by going out on a limb, it has paid dividends.

The JC twist

When you are a candidate sitting in front of the employer, the fact that you don't have the perfect CV doesn't mean you can't do the job. There is no such thing as the perfect candidate. As long as you display your experience to its best advantage and match it as carefully as you can to the needs of the job, you have done as much as you can in advance. On the day it could be that extra flash of passion that makes *all* the difference.

'Creating your CV is not about going through the motions according to a tired old formula. It is your chance to sell yourself and, above all, to get that vital first interview.'

3. PACKAGING

If you look at what the abbreviation CV stands for – 'curriculum vitae', the Latin for 'the course of a life' – or if you think of the alternative word 'résumé' that is popular in the States, the whole document could sound rather old-fashioned, even quaint, and unsuited for the demands of the twenty-first century. You couldn't be further from the truth.

When you are looking for a holiday, what makes you choose a particular destination, resort, hotel or villa over an equally good alternative? You usually know as soon as you find one that offers not only what you need, but then something extra. An employer or recruiter is looking for exactly the same thing. Writing a winning CV is all about creating one that – everything else being equal – gives *you* an advantage.

The CV is still the most efficient and effective way of putting yourself in the frame for a job. But as with everything in this book, that in itself is not enough. There is a way of using this basic weapon and turning it from an unsophisticated bludgeon, banging away with facts that have no value or relevance in the context of landing a job, into a deft rapier, elegantly conveying the critical information, and getting straight to the point.

A question of delivery

How many times do you hear in business that 'it is all about delivery'? I am going to turn this chapter right on its head. Let's assume you have already created a great CV – and later we will come to how you do that. What you want is for that CV, which you have, or which more accurately you *should* have, spent a lot of time on is ready to go. How can you best make sure that your CV is seen by the person who is going to call you and ask you to come in for an interview?

Let me put that another way. **How do you think ninety per cent of all CVs are delivered?**

Answer: by email. Only ten per cent are delivered in the post. Ten years ago the answer would have been the exact opposite.

At that time, sending in your CV by email would have made you stand out precisely because it was unusual. Now it makes you one of the masses. Which means that your CV, however brilliant in content, is competing with a raft of other CVs that probably look very similar to yours.

It certainly works for me. Since virtually everything comes to me by email, whenever my PA hands me my post tray at work I actually read it, because it contains less and, for some strange reason, it seems more important. I can't read all the emails in my in-box, because there are too many. That's why I get a digest of all the emails that have come in for me.

I am sure most people do not have time to read through every email they get. You always hear about people coming back into their office after a couple of weeks away on holiday, and spending their first week back doing very little other than ploughing through the backlog in their in-box, most of which is either irrelevant or redundant because it is already out of date, junk mail or spam. Imagine what it's like in an HR department where they get masses and masses of emailed CVs.

It is always worth taking some time to track down the name of the person within the company who will actually be making the hiring decision. If the job ad indicates that the role on offer will be reporting to the marketing director, but doesn't give that person's name, then you may get lucky straight away by looking at the staff profiles on the company's website. If that doesn't work, try entering 'marketing director' and the company name into Google. That might throw up an article they have written, a newspaper interview, the announcement in the trade press about them getting that job. Nine times out of ten, some astute and persistent searching will turn up the snippet of information that you need.

But if none of those online options work, then you can go back to some straightforward old-fashioned sleuthing! I was always ringing up switchboards to get names. My standard line used to be, 'Oh, hi, I'm just dropping a letter to the production director. Could you let me have his name, please?' or, 'I'd like to contact somebody who looks after export sales. Who should

I write to?' Reception or security would nearly always tell me without even asking who I was. And it still works – in those jobs turnover is often high, and somebody who's only been in the job for a few weeks or months usually hasn't been inducted into giving nothing away. Even with the wonderful power of the Web, the old-school techniques are just as effective as they ever were.

Lesson Number One: if you have the name of the decision maker for a job, rather than a generic HR executive, and you want to send them your CV, send it by post (alongside any formal online application you are asked to make). Because you'll be one of the few who do.

That's a good step forward, because it automatically picks you out. Now ask yourself another question. **What can I do that will make my CV stand out even more than sending it by post?**

Answer: deliver it by hand.

When you walk into a company's reception area and hand-deliver a letter, what happens? It doesn't get put in the post tray with the letters. It gets hand-delivered in turn to the person it is addressed to.

Imagine you have decided to hand-deliver a CV to me. The point is not hand-delivering it to me personally; the point is you want to get my attention. So, if you think about how to do it, you will not deliver the CV first thing in the morning. If you do that, you have blown your chance, because the letter will be mixed in with my post tray. However, by 11 a.m. I have already received my post.

If you come in at midday, bypassing all the processes, and say, 'Hi, I've got a letter for James Caan,' what do you think would happen? Yes, somebody will come straight down and bring it up to me, but the critical aspect is that the letter will be given to me on its own. It is not part of a wodge of correspondence. Again, what do you think I'm going to do? I'm going to open it.

Lesson Number Two: if you really want your CV to be noticed, hand-deliver it. It's a question of ranking. If you want to be right at the top of the pile, hand-deliver it. The second-best option is to send it by post; the least effective option is to email it. A job ad will say, 'Send all CVs by email.' You can do that: it costs you nothing, no effort, to email it in. But if it was me, I would hand-deliver it every time.

Again, because most CVs have been created following a rather rigid template, anything you can do to lift its profile is valuable. The CV you are sending in could be one of a hundred, one of 500, one of over a thousand.

If you think of the person at the other end going through a hundred CVs, ask yourself why they would remember your CV. If you want to put it on black paper with white writing, do it, because you only have seconds to capture their imagination and their attention. I would always prefer a CV to stand out and get noticed, rather than get buried.

When that person opens your CV, unless there is something about it that is screaming off the page – a sentence, a word, a look, a colour, a picture – the only button it's going to push is the 'Delete' one.

I realize that this goes against the grain of received wisdom: that employers and HR departments do not like weird presentations and wacky layouts, and may reject CVs that are not straightforward and conventional. As you might have realized by now, I am not always convinced that the straightforward, conventional route is the best.

Depending on the job sector you are in, and the job you are applying for, you could consider adding a video clip: certainly this is an option which recruitment specialists are certain will grow over the next ten years. Already companies are offering online platforms for video CVs: there are a number of websites which make it possible for candidates to plan, film and post video CVs and for employers to view them. I invested in One Way Resourcing, an online recruitment business for the construction industry that harnesses the power of video clips. But until it becomes commonplace, the video clip still has the great advantage of novelty. You will certainly be ahead of the masses.

It depends on the relevance for the job. For the sake of argument, if the job you are applying for is as an accounts assistant, I would probably not send a video clip – it doesn't seem appropriate – but if the job is in a media or marketing agency, and a video clip might prompt them to say, 'That shows creativity!' why not? You could send your CV with the video clip as an extra. That way you are covering your options. If they don't open the clip, they still have the CV, and if they do open the clip they have the advantage of watching it.

Within that clip, you could provide a sixty-second intro:

'Hi, I'm James, thanks for reading my CV. I just want to take this opportunity of introducing myself: this is what I've done.' There is no question that people get drawn in by an image.

In a job market where jobs are few but candidates are many, and where most of those candidates are highly qualified and at the same level, the differentials in terms of experience between all the CVs received for a job will even out. The whole objective comes down to: why you? That is why these differences – such as how you deliver a CV – become significantly more important. That must be Step One of the recruitment process. You know that the job you want is one that 500 other people also want. The chances are the majority of them have the same things to offer as you do. So, you need to position yourself ahead of the pack.

Absolutely everything at this stage of the process is in your power – whether that's hand-delivering the CV, creating a podcast, sending copies of press articles about yourself – just as it is totally within your power to research using the Web, to learn about the company, to understand the competition.

Any imaginative, inventive approach, something with an ounce of wit, will tweak my interest. Somebody was pitching me a business idea in the clothes trade and hand-delivered me a suit. Of course I tried it on, and I was shocked. It was exactly my size. Simply because of that I had to call the guy because it fitted perfectly. I was surprised that he had managed to get my measurements so right.

I called and said, 'I got your business plan, thanks for the suit. Can I ask you the question, "How did you guess my size?"'

He said, 'I went on to Google Images and looked at the pictures of you. You have to remember, James, I do this for a living. I can generally estimate a man's height. I imagine you're about 5 ft 8 ins' – which is exactly what I am – 'and about a size 40.' He was right. He got everything – waist, chest, inside leg – spot on. I remembered that my dad, who manufactured leather garments, could do the same thing; he could look at you and tell your measurements without measuring you. This guy pitching me the suit business *could* have sent me a suit in any size, but he had worked out that if he sent one in *my* size, the chances are that I would try it on. And he got the required result – I called him direct.

The JC twist

When candidates fail to get an interview, they never assume it was their fault. They immediately think, 'The company probably had too many CVs,' or, 'I didn't fit the profile.' They blame it on something else, whereas I don't think that's necessarily the case. The employer has a problem. They have a job vacancy, and every day that vacancy goes unfilled, it loses them money. If I am advertising for a job, it is because I am desperate. I need somebody in that role. If you happen to have the right experience, that job is yours to lose, because I am shouting from the rooftops, 'I have a problem,' and you are the solution. If you have not communicated that you are my solution, then go back and review what you have been saying in your CV.

What are the secrets of an effective CV?

Remember that the person who you want to hire you will spend no more than a few seconds, a couple of minutes tops, scanning your CV, so it has to be impressive, and instantly effective. It's exactly like *Dragons' Den*: each entrepreneur has only a matter of minutes to pitch themselves to the Dragons to guarantee an investor's interest. This time the product is you.

There is no room for a finely worded, beautifully composed story of the ins and outs and ups and downs of your career. You need to present your experience, strengths, skills and ambitions in a short, accessible package: minimum two pages, maximum three. Anything longer is not going to be read. In fact, most decision makers say they want to know immediately, from the first page alone, that there is a positive match between the job and the candidate, and really don't want to dig any further.

When you are writing a CV, the first thing you need to ask yourself is, 'What is the job I'm applying for?' Most people write generic CVs. Now, bearing in mind that the employer is looking for a specific candidate with a specific skill set, when faced with a generic CV the employer has to read the whole of the CV to try and find the appropriate match, by which time they have generally become bored. CVs are cold pieces of paper which have no life. No one is going to spend too much time reading them.

My impression is that most people think that a CV is a formal document, some kind of legal document. It is not – although you should not lie on your CV. There have been cases where successful prosecutions, with a prison sentence to boot, have been brought against applicants making fraudulent claims.

And there lies the immediate observation: legal documents are not designed to sell. A CV is a marketing document, it is a sales document. Think of it as building Brand You. The CV is designed to sell *you* as a candidate to an employer, to grab their interest from the word go, to entice them into hiring you.

I realized this when my own daughters were preparing their personal statements for university, and later their first CVs. They were too long, too wordy, there was too much information that was not relevant. My own children! I had probably thought that by living with me all their lives, they would have automatically, instinctively acquired the knowledge of how to create the right document by osmosis. But I realized they hadn't – because I hadn't ever told them how to do it. They, just like anybody else, needed to understand the approach and the techniques required. So, I explained the concept by saying, 'If this was called a "Sell Jemma" or a "Sell Hanah" document, you would position it differently. Keep the word "sell" in your head every minute you sit there writing it.' I must admit I spent a lot of time with both of them, reworking their first versions, helping them focus on the areas of their experience that were directly relevant either to the degree they wanted to study, or the job they wanted to get.

Make your CV work for you, by making sure that the way you list your experience highlights what you bring to the table. The analogy I like to use is that it's a bit like the grocer: your best apples have got to be at the front. I am not a fan of endless bullet points listing generic duties that have been copied and pasted from a job description. They are pretty meaningless, since they could apply to anybody doing that job.

In the same way, setting out your 'career objectives' has little value – from an employer's point of view I am actually expecting and hoping that your next key career objective is getting this job you have just applied for. I don't need to know any more than that.

I always want to see how you *personally* have added value to your existing employer's business, by increasing sales, improving staff performance or coming up with innovative ideas that have opened up new markets. What are your USPs, why should a new company invest its money in hiring you?

When I first set up the Alexander Mann recruitment agency, in 1985, I was operating out of a tiny, windowless, claustrophobic office. I spent a month phoning hundreds of different companies and getting nowhere – and I finally realized I was using the same pitch to every client. I had to tailor my pitch. If my client had an engineering or science background I would cut through the flannel and serve up information with hard facts and figures. If it was a relationship advice service I'd emphasize how my previous work had benefited other people. You should tailor your CV to the personality of the company you are applying to. Each CV you create should be a bespoke item.

In the recruitment business, time was when agencies had a typing pool where all candidates' CVs were rewritten and squeezed into the same format – that attitude still prevails in the agencies who like to send out CVs in a standard format that is really designed to promote the agency's own identity and branding. The more enlightened agencies have realized that it makes more sense to allow a candidate to produce an individual CV that allows their own style and approach to emerge naturally rather than being straitjacketed into some kind of corporate uniform. Taking the time to create a CV specific to each job tells an employer that you have a genuine interest in the position.

My recommendation is that you design a generic CV to give yourself a framework and, depending on the job you're applying for, personalize that CV. Let's say you've seen the vacancy on a job board, or in a newspaper advert. What you're trying to do is read into the job, understand what they're looking for, and make sure that either in the highlights of your career, or in your covering note, you have captured the correlation or the link with the vacancy. The critical elements are – usually – obvious from the job specification and the job ad.

At Hamilton Bradshaw we were advertising for an investment director. The ad we ran stated quite clearly that we were handling deals worth up to £10 million. Of the CVs that came in as a result of the ad, almost all of them said, 'I've done deals at £400 million, £800 million, a billion pounds.' On that alone we discounted those CVs. We did not even process them because we felt those candidates were irrelevant for our purposes. If you were coming from an environment where you were executing billion-pound leverage deals, what relevance did that have to Hamilton Bradshaw? But each of these CVs had that fact right up front because the candidates thought it was a key selling point. In fact that worked completely against them because it proved they had not read the job spec or tried to match their experience to it.

It would only have taken a small amount of think-time for one of those candidates to change the message to one with a different slant: 'I have the experience, I have the right background, I have been in financial services and I am sure I could do the job.' Any candidate who did have the background and experience and who had taken the trouble to rewrite his CV along those lines would probably have found themselves called in for an interview.

That is clear evidence of the fact that jobs are not generic. Companies are not generic. People are not generic.

A CV does not have to follow a particular pattern, even though there are certain elements that are givens. There is no grid that you must follow. Writing a CV is not a science. It requires judgement. It needs intuition.

In all aspects of your CV, highlighting the relevant information is critical. In your educational information, for example, you can list a barrage of GCSEs, A Levels, degrees and other qualifications, but if you actually got 6 A*s, I think you should say you've got 6 A*s because, to me, the message that comes across loud and clear is that even at a young age this candidate was a straight-A* person. But don't make me spend my time searching for that information. The more I have to look for it, the chances are I've lost interest. Mentally I am making decisions in seconds, not minutes. Just like a computer I am scanning your CV and wordsearching it. If my brain is not identifying with the words, or the words that are coming up are irrelevant to what

I want, I will simply move the CV to one side. It really is that straightforward. This applies to anything that you have done in your career which makes you stand out: that particular piece of information should be right at the front.

This avoids the most common problem with CVs: most people go into too much detail. Their CV is too micro. Overlong spiels, especially those full of marketing or industry jargon, send out a negative message suggesting lack of focus. A CV should be simpler, more highlight driven – and those highlights should be those aspects of your career and experience that make a positive contribution to the position that you are applying for, and are relevant to the company that you are targeting.

Keep asking yourself: **Is this piece of information relevant to me getting this job?**

When you set out your employment record, review each position you have had for its relevance to the job on offer. In the event that you had a job that was completely irrelevant, it does not matter for the purpose of the CV. You can add it in as a one-liner, because if there is any value in it for the employer, that will come up in the interview.

The same applies to your education. Always consider the relevance. If you have only been working for five years, your education still represents a large chunk of who you are. If I am looking at the CV of a 25-year-old, I will always go into that aspect. Which school did you go to? What were your grades? What were you thinking when you took that particular degree? Tell me a bit about the syllabus. Because that is all relevant to me; it tells me how you think. But if you have been working for thirty-five years, that part of your life is too far away; it has lost its value. Better to include examples of recent or additional qualifications, which demonstrate a continued commitment to learning and self-improvement.

If you are new to the job market, and do not yet have experience in the workplace under your belt, you can look at activities that show specific values. If you are captain of a local sports team, that indicates leadership potential. And this is where the value of work experience and internships comes into play, and helps put you on a more equal footing.

The laws covering which elements of information can or cannot be included in a CV have grown over the last decade. If you are working with a recruitment agency, they will be up to speed on the niceties, or you can check the Department for Business, Innovation & Skills website for the same details.

I believe that personal information should be included because it can be quite pertinent: whether you have a family, whether you have young children. Certain jobs require travelling or unsocial hours, and inevitably this is going to be a question which you will be asked during the interview.

If you have personal interests which are relevant, again put them in as one-liners. It's a matter of personal preference. If they are not connected or associated with the job, or could even be detrimental, I am not sure why you would want to include them. I am personally usually less than enthused to learn that you like 'socializing, the cinema and cooking', unless there is a direct relevance to the job on offer.

Generally I am not bothered about knowing you enjoy

reading, for example – but if I was a publisher and you were coming in for a job as an editorial assistant, I would not only expect to read that, but I would also expect you to be able to answer a simple question such as 'What books do you enjoy reading?' How difficult is it for you to work out that I am going to ask you that question? I am not going to be impressed by you sitting there looking flummoxed when I toss you such a gimme of a question. If you do put down a personal interest that is pertinent to the job, make sure you are ready to talk about it intelligently and relevantly.

When you have completed your CV, step back from it for a while, so that you can give yourself a sense of perspective as you review the information it contains and the highlights you have selected. Put yourself in the place of a prospective employer and read it with their mindset uppermost in your thoughts. Make a checklist of the core elements of the original job ad and cross-check that the CV you have created identifies your strengths in each of those elements, and does it quickly and clearly. Ask yourself: is your CV succinct, targeted, factual, accurate and simple?

If you think you need additional help, there are – naturally – online CV review and critique services. It certainly helps to have a dispassionate view – you may be too close to the finished document to make a clear judgement.

Sometimes the obvious gets forgotten precisely because it is so obvious. Recently I got a letter from someone who was working in the retail sector. He said that he enjoyed working in retail, was able to get jobs at the lower end of the ladder with ease, and would usually be promoted within companies he was working for. But whenever he applied for a role in management, he never got an interview. Here was someone driven, focused, enthusiastic – but what was the one thing he had forgotten to mention in his CV? He had been promoted four times in one particular year, and he didn't put that in. No wonder he was not being called in for an interview.

What about the covering letter?

A covering letter is a much undervalued part of the CV package. Some candidates don't even bother – which can lead to their CV going straight in the bin. Or they treat it as an extra hassle. I have seen many, many covering letters that are bland, unthinking and careless.

Think of the covering letter as an additional platform to sell yourself and your suitability for the job.

The letter should be short and to the point (some employers also like it to be handwritten as it shows personal style and that you can spell without the help of a spellchecker). Two paragraphs should do the trick: paragraph A would be the details of the requirements for the job, and paragraph B would be why you have exactly that experience and can rise to those challenges.

Focus on the key words you picked up from the advert or the job spec or the online description. If I read a covering letter that says, 'I am responding to the job of Finance Director that you advertised, running a department of six people,' almost repeating what I have said in the advert, those words are ringing bells in my head, because they are my own words. Naturally it will sound right to me, because you are telling me what I want to hear.

Extract the guts of the job and put those into the covering note, and you will be right on message. The hirer will understand that you know exactly what the job is. To me that is automatically a positive.

The JC twist

Rather than hiding away while you chisel your CV to perfection, ask a friend or a colleague to read it and give you their thoughts. Get over any sense of embarrassment, and look at the benefits. Your friend is much more likely to pick up on a strength or achievement you've overlooked – it's very difficult to be objective about yourself.

Asking for feedback

If you are applying for a number of jobs at the same level over a certain time period, why not get feedback on your CV in the course of the interview? When you are asked if you have any questions, say, 'I am delighted to be here. Can you tell me, what was it about my CV that you found interesting? Was there anything you have learned in this interview that you would have liked to see in the CV?' People will happily tell you there and then.

As you move forward to the next job opportunity, you can perfect your CV, tailor it again based on those comments. Practice makes perfect. Even very senior managers can always improve their CVs. How many times do Rafael Nadal and Roger Federer hit the ball in a practice session? And does that have any relevance to why they are great sportsmen? How many times has David Beckham kicked that ball to curve it round a wall into the net? Do you think he only did it once? No, he kicked it again and again and again, to get better and better. The process here is no different.

You will reap the rewards of the time and effort you put into creating the very best CV you can. Your CV is a potential passport to success – it could bring you a job you will be in for the next ten years. It could be the job that changes your life, the job that brings you to your next big opportunity. Of course it is worth the investment.

Do not skimp on any effort at this stage. Because in today's world, getting the interview is everything. Job hunting is a process. If you take Stage One, you need to get your CV in front of the hiring manager and get him or her to see you. And in that component, why compromise? Because if you fail at that, there is no process. If you don't get the call, you are out of the game, and you will never have the opportunity to move on to Stage Two: the interview itself.

"This next job could transform your life. So, why try and busk the interview? If you research and prepare to the very best of your ability, you will go in with palpable confidence and a massive advantage."

4. PREPARATION

Even after all the hours I have spent listening to pitches in the Dragons' Den, I am still amazed at how many of these otherwise bright and talented entrepreneurs do not understand the importance of good competitor analysis. If you don't know your competitors, you are going to fail – no question. Yet time and time again, when I and the other Dragons question them about what other products are on the market, they simply don't know.

That's why, of the people who enter the Dragons' Den, ninety per cent fail. And the reason is simple: they did not do the right research. They did not do their homework. Therefore they come in and they flounder. We sit there, horrified. We genuinely do not know who is going to walk through the door next, but these entrepreneurs know that this event could change their lives. But even so, they still don't prepare properly. It's unbelievable.

More often than not – surprise, surprise – those who do their research end up walking away with an investment. Each entrepreneur has no more than twenty minutes to persuade us to make a decision in their favour. The decision we make is based on the confidence we pick up on. If you can stand there, hold your ground, know your numbers, and communicate that information to us articulately and convincingly, you stand a very good chance of securing an investment.

The equivalent of this in the job market is not so much knowing your direct competitors, the other applicants – it's more than likely you will never know who the other applicants are and, in any case, you should go into the interview believing you are the right person for the job – but you must have done your research on the company you are applying to work for, just as though they were a business competitor. This time the goal is not an investment to move your business on, but the chance to land the job you really want. **With that golden incentive, why would you not bother doing the research?**

Coming at the same question from a related angle, when I was first asked to go on *Dragons' Den*, what do you suppose was the very first thing I did when the production team approached me? I asked them to send me a set of DVDs with the last ten episodes of the show. To me that was the natural thing to do. I thought to myself, 'I have never done any television. I'm not part of that world, and I know nothing about it. In order for me to even understand what it is I am supposed to be doing, I should watch and learn.'

And I did. I spent one entire weekend watching all the episodes back to back. The result: when I went along to do my trial rehearsal, I found it was not that difficult – or certainly far less difficult than I might have imagined – simply because I had watched ten hours of the show. I knew exactly what the format was. I knew exactly what kind of questions the Dragons asked. I understood what the dynamics between the other Dragons were. It had become pretty obvious, because I had carried out the right preparation, the right research.

When I was in the recruitment business, way before *Dragons' Den*, I was frequently astonished by how little preparation applicants had undertaken before an interview for a job. They had only the skimpiest knowledge of a company's background and had certainly never thought to check up on recent developments within the field.

Preparation, preparation, preparation

I cannot emphasize enough how important a factor serious preparation and research is in getting the job you want. It is the passport to bigger and better things. You would think it was an obvious thing to do before any interview, but, as with so many aspects of this process, a remarkably high number of candidates, even at a very senior level, fail to do it.

How many finance directors go for an interview and beforehand do a search on the company and pull out their accounts? Hardly any. Over the years I have interviewed many dozens, probably hundreds, of finance directors, and I am yet to interview one who has come in to see me carrying a copy of my accounts. What does it cost to procure somebody's accounts? A fiver, and very little effort – go to Companies House, tap in the name of the company, download them.

When I am interviewing a finance director, I am trying to evaluate whether or not he or she can do the job – and not in some abstract, academic way. I want to know whether they can do the job specifically for my company. If the candidate had taken the trouble to download my accounts, they would know what my turnover in the last reporting year was, what my profits were. And armed with that information, if they are good at what they do, they will have the raw material to engage in an intellectual dialogue with me. If I am going to assess them on their specialist subject – finance – what better environment in which to have that conversation than the one I know a lot about: my own numbers? And what a great opportunity for a candidate to engage with me.

If I went for an interview as a finance director, I would read the accounts in advance and analyse the financial state and the business trends of the company, and as a result I would be able to hold my own in any conversation about its finances. Without trying too hard, I would have had a very good impact on the interviewer.

There's a balance to be struck here. You want to be well informed, but take care not to overload the interviewer with statistics and details about their own company. They want you to be interested, not obsessive. Use the information you have gleaned to raise points for discussion in the interview – this shows interest and intellect.

In an interview what really impresses me are those candidates who have shown initiative. I really admire people who have invested their own time in finding out whether they would be an ideal fit within the company, because – after all – it is not just down to the employer.

How many times have I asked someone who has come in for an interview, 'What do you know about Hamilton Bradshaw?' and they have answered, 'Not a great deal,' or they start off but dry up after a few seconds? At least fifty per cent of the time. There is no reason on God's earth for you to be caught out like this at an interview, absolutely no excuse.

For me personally, when I ask that question and discover that the candidate has very little knowledge about Hamilton Bradshaw, in my head I am thinking, 'You have blown at least fifty per cent of your overall score.' If you wanted this job, if this job meant enough to you, that is the very least you should have done. The fact that you *didn't* bother doing it – and what that tells me about you both as a professional and as a person – does not impress me.

In the past this would not have been a big issue. Today it is, because all of that information is so easily accessible. The tools are readily at your disposal.

One of the significant changes in the job-hunting process over the past ten to fifteen years has been the arrival of the phenomenal power of the internet, not just in terms of being able to find job opportunities on job boards and through online recruitment agencies, but in terms of the access it provides to a huge amount of information that is in the public domain and can be discovered in a few clicks.

You can research most prospective companies by starting with their website. I don't mean spending five minutes on the morning of the interview having a quick look at the home page while still munching a piece of toast – although, unbelievably, many, if not most, candidates do not even bother doing that bare minimum of preparation.

Every company has a website, every company has a whole stack of information. It is a gateway to their way of doing business, their beliefs, their mentality, their whole personality.

If you were coming in for that interview at Hamilton Bradshaw, and you tapped 'Hamilton Bradshaw' into Google, you would be able to find, from our site alone, all of the deals that we have done, the companies we've invested in, press articles on individual investment directors, plus media coverage of all our activities. Company websites contain press releases on new product launches, Careers sections listing current job vacancies – both of which will tell you which areas they are actively expanding into. You can find out their office locations and their staffing levels. All this is publicly available information that would be incredibly valuable to you as reference material in the interview.

If you really want the job, scanning the website is not enough. You actually have to spend quality time on the site, studying it in detail. Get out your notepad, and take notes.

- In which year was the company established?
- How many people does it employ?
- What is its core market?
- Geographically, where are its strengths?
- What is its product range?
- Who are the company's key competitors?

You can learn all this from the information available on the internet. Carrying out this fundamental research will allow you to walk into the interview a little bit taller, because you will be more confident.

So, this time, when I ask you – as I *always* will – the question, 'What do you know about Hamilton Bradshaw?' you should be in there straight away – bang! – 'I understand you were established in 2004, you have a team of x people, you focus on these markets, your average deal size is this.' You should know these facts instantly.

But also try to go beyond the pure facts. Look at the broader context. Try and read between the lines and create an insight into the personality of the company you want to join. Take time to learn about the whole range of a company's values, read their corporate/social responsibility mission statement, and aim to glean something of their corporate culture. If their shares are listed, how have the shares been performing, and what do business journalists think about that performance? Read recent copies of the relevant trade press, in print or online (where you may also find some pertinent bloggers with a different take not only on the sector you work in but also on the company you are interested in) to find out how they are perceived within the industry.

You should quickly get a feel of any relevant trends, how the company is performing against their competitors, what their major initiatives are and any significant achievements in the previous couple of years. Many recruitment companies now ask candidates, as part of their overall preparation, to draw up a SWOT (strengths, weaknesses, opportunities, threats) analysis of the company they are applying to join. You can do that off your own bat.

I also find that reading press interviews with, or profiles of, the chief executive, the managing director – at the very least you should know who both of them are, and what they have achieved – and other senior managers often provides you with a sense of the company's attitudes, expressed in a natural way that you can reword and rework in the interview to convey those attitudes without sounding like you're regurgitating last year's company report. Along the way you can pick up phrases or buzzwords that you can identify with when you are talking about your own experience.

Beyond the internet, use any other network available to you.

Talk to people you know, or friends of friends, who have worked with or for the company – you'll get some great information straight away. It is essential to embrace technology, but there is nothing quite like picking up the phone or having a face-to-face chat to glean unexpected titbits of information outside the preprogrammed algorithms of a search engine.

If somebody approaches me with a product for investment, I will always go out and talk to retailers who would be likely to stock that product. I find they nearly always give me one piece of vital information I would never otherwise have picked up.

And finally, if you know who is going to interview you, research that person. Look to see if they have a short biography on their company website or, even better, a profile on LinkedIn, so that you can see how they personally developed their career. Again, there may be press pieces about them online. If there's a photo of them, add it to your file of research. The fewer surprises the better. And you will pick up some background details that might give you a couple of ideas for small talk before and after the interview.

Beware... Just as you may be researching your interviewer online, you should assume that they or their colleagues are doing exactly the same about you. Bring your LinkedIn profile up to date and check that it matches your CV. If you have a presence on Facebook or MySpace, take a long hard look at it. Have you spent rather too much time telling your friends just how much you hate your boss, or the amount of time you've been bunking off work to meet up with your mates? And make sure there are absolutely no embarrassing YouTube clips of you from the last office party!

Preparation – whether it's researching on the Web, downloading information, studying accounts, doing competitor analysis, or talking to former colleagues – is fundamental to the job-finding process. It is absolutely critical. I would almost say that if you haven't done the research, don't bother turning up for the interview.

But if you have done the right preparation – and if you have done it well – when the shortlist is being drawn up, the company will remember you as the applicant who put in an extraordinary amount of effort and work.

This was a lesson I had to learn. When I first started work, I didn't know any of this. I had no concept of the importance of preparation and research. In the beginning I relied too heavily on force of personality, rather than substance. When I walked into an interview, I tried to wing it. And as a result my hit rate was not that good. I might have gone for seven or eight different interviews in order to land one job. But each time I changed jobs, I tried to learn from the previous experience and improve my attitude. Part of this was the fact that I didn't really know what kind of career I wanted to pursue. I had an idea in my mind, but I couldn't identify what it was. If you'd asked me when I left school which industry I would go into, recruitment would have been the last one on my list. In fact, it wouldn't even have been on my list, because I didn't know what it was. When my first job didn't work out, I moved on to another sector, and each time I changed jobs

I got a little closer to where I was going. Sometimes, in order to find the right destination, you need to try out some different avenues.

The JC twist

This might surprise you: if you have done all this research and preparation on my company, I really don't mind if you have not learned that information by heart. If you have a set of notes in front of you and read off those notes, I am totally relaxed about that. A series of keywords to prompt you would be better, but either way I would not mind. Most people's perception is that they have to memorize everything. There is no rule written down anywhere which states, 'You must memorize the facts.' If, during the interview, you ask, 'Would you mind if I use some notes?' most people will be quite comfortable with you taking out your research.

I have had candidates who have downloaded my entire website and I can see that they have gone through the pages with a highlighter pen. Do you know what? If you did that, I would be impressed. Even though you have the information right there in front of you, I would mentally still give you the same score as a candidate who had memorized it. And the fact that you have highlighted key sections shows me more: that you have thought about the relevance of information on the site. You might think these little details are unimportant. I rate them very highly.

The information you acquire from your research provides you with a level of currency. You will make even more progress if you can improve its value. So, if you have found out who a company's main competitors are, and how those competitors perform, you can convert that knowledge into a question in the interview: 'I noticed, James, that one of your competitors is X. They happen to be twice the size of this company. What is it about what they do that has enabled them to achieve that?' This is an excellent question that demonstrates not just knowledge, but the confidence to ask the interviewer a relevant but challenging question – and by asking it the balance of power has automatically shifted towards you, the candidate.

Taking the test

If you want to give yourself some extra advantage, you could, under your own steam, take a psychometric or personality profile test. Many companies, especially those which are more sophisticated and more technology driven, ask job candidates to undergo these tests as a matter of course. Fifteen or twenty years ago, although they existed, these tests were seen as slightly mysterious, and a little bit wacky, but now they are commonplace.

I certainly have found them useful as an employer, because they often tell me a little bit more than the interview, and they can help clarify a particular issue that has emerged in the process, resolve some conflicting impression, or suggest areas to probe in a second or third interview.

But you don't need to wait until the company asks you. There are plenty of tests available online that you can take yourself. For a relatively low level of outlay – anywhere between £25 and £100 – you can find a specific personality profile test for your kind of job function, which would present you in a relevant light for the position you are applying for. You go online, answer the multiple-choice questions, put your credit card details in, and the site automatically generates a report for you.

Some observers believe you can skew the results by recognizing the questions, but it's best not to try and second-guess the test. Answer straightforwardly and honestly, using your gut feeling, and if the job you are applying for is the right one for you and your particular experience and skills, you should find no major surprises in the results, only positive comments.

Imagine if you came in for the second interview and said, 'By the way, James, I recently took a test in terms of my skills and characteristics which I thought you might find useful.' That would be quite a neat thing to do. As the employer I may have been considering giving you a similar test – but you've not only shown initiative, you have hand-delivered the test to me ready wrapped. And of course you are only going to give me those test results if they say all the things you want to say.

Is it worth rehearsing for an interview?

As part of your preparation some rehearsal time is valuable. You know that certain standard questions are always going to be asked of you.

'Why do you want to leave your current employer?'

'What do you know about this company?'

'Are there any questions you would like to ask?'

Think through your answers to these predictable questions, and then try to phrase them in a natural and conversational, rather than robotic, way.

There will be sections of the interview where your response may not be straightforward. There may be certain issues that you are uncomfortable with. Maybe you have a gap in your CV: the interviewer will pick up on that. Perhaps you left a job too quickly, after only six months, or maybe you were in a job for too *long*: the interviewer will home in on that.

Rehearsing the answers to these difficult questions will always prove useful, because if you do not prepare them, you will tend to become rather defensive under pressure during the interview. At that point you are at your most vulnerable, your most uncomfortable. If you are dealing with an experienced interviewer, they will know that, and inevitably, whenever they see a chink in your armour, any sign of weakness, they will zero in on it, because they are trying to get under your skin.

I know, because I have done it many, many times. The chances are that if you have not prepared in advance what you are going to say in response to the awkward questions, you are going to lose the job by saying something off the top of your head which, in retrospect, may turn out not to be the smartest thing to say.

Under those circumstances I think it is extremely useful to have a dummy run. If you are working with a good recruitment consultant, they will be able to rehearse with you. Or you can practise your answers with a friend or colleague, a partner, parent, brother or sister, or a flat-mate – and then ask them how each answer sounds to their ears. Is it convincing? Is it too defensive? Does it raise other questions?

The knack is not to learn your answers word for word. That starts to sound more like a script. And – how annoying! – your interviewer won't have a copy of that script. If you are relying too much on prepared answers, any questions that are unscripted can throw you off your stride. You should be aiming at *consistency* of answers, but phrasing them differently each time.

In the lead-up to the 2010 General Election, and the first-ever prime ministerial debates in the UK – a job interview held in front of millions of viewers – imagine the number of times David Cameron, Nick Clegg and Gordon Brown rehearsed their answers to questions on the economy, on immigration, on foreign policy. They all knew that there were two other people who wanted the job of prime minister as much, if not more, than they did and would be looking for weaknesses, for openings. To perform well, they would have to be completely on top of their game, because everything they said was going to be over-analysed in the following days. Therefore, what did they do? They practised, they rehearsed, they got colleagues to act the part of the other leaders. They did everything they could to ensure that the responses they gave to all the questions they might reasonably expect to be asked addressed the points raised, conveyed the message they wanted the electorate to hear, and were as watertight as they could make them.

It does not matter what the job is, there is always somebody else who really wants that job. You should be thinking, 'What are the other candidates doing in preparation? **Why do they want that job more than I do?'**

You need to prepare more than they do, be more ready than they are. Whether you are trying to land a job as a prime minister, as a sales assistant or as a CEO, there is actually no difference. It is all relative.

Of course, all of this preparation takes time. So, you need to build the necessary time into your schedule in the period available before an interview. If you do not do that, you can predict the outcome. It is true of most of the things we do – not just getting a job – that with anything you do well, the chances are you will succeed.

Anything you do in a rushed, unplanned, disorganized, haphazard way – lack of preparation, lack of planning, lack of presentation – chances are it will result in nothing. I have learned that in business, time and time again. Strangely enough, the things that work out well are those things that you prepare for and carry out with commitment and care.

'The kind of people I like to employ
are smart in all senses of the word:
they think smart, they act smart,
and they look smart, professional
and prepared.'

5. PRESENTATION

In the early 1990s a couple of psychologists at Harvard set up a deceptively simple experiment. Three separate groups were shown footage of one of the faculty's staff members giving a lecture. The first of these groups was shown a ten-second clip of him, the second group a five-second segment, the final group only two seconds. Then each group had to evaluate the lecturer's aptitude.

Believe it or not, the evaluations from each group were identical. Think about what that means. Just two seconds – 'Mississippi one, Mississippi two', no longer than that – is enough time for somebody to form a lasting impression. So, if you make a bad impression on me in the opening two seconds of our meeting, whatever you do in the following eight seconds is irrelevant. I will still start off classing you as a no-hoper. Sorry to be so blunt, but it's true. I have an immediate perception of somebody when they walk in, and that first look sets the tone for the remainder of the interview.

Irrespective of what other people might say or think, I personally believe that presentation ranks very highly, because those first impressions are very hard to change. As part of your preparation for a job interview you should be continually reviewing how you will come across – and not just physically, but mentally and emotionally too.

Whether you like it or not, people will judge you on the way you look. You have to accept that the judgement can go against you. My question is always this: 'Why would you take the risk?'

Setting out your stall

Everything about you is like a shop window – how you look, sound, present yourself, walk, speak, what briefcase or bag you are carrying when you walk into the interview. Each of these forms part of the overall window display. **If you are not prepared to invest in the way you display yourself, why should you expect to be successful?**

When I first set up my recruitment company Alexander Mann, I persuaded the rather sniffy manageress of a serviced office building in Pall Mall to let me rent a minuscule office there. I would always meet clients in the impressive entrance hall and suggest that we nip out for a coffee to chat. I would tell them there were far too many people upstairs to have a proper private talk, or something along those lines. The reality was that my tiny office was so awful I didn't want anyone to see it. The ploy worked, and I definitely owe some of my success to that building's splendid exterior. So, although superficial gloss cannot achieve success on its own – there has to be some serious substance behind it – you can still make sure you present the best exterior possible.

I heard a great piece of advice recently: when you're going for an interview, don't try to be the *perfect* candidate – that is an impossibility – but just make sure you're better than everyone else who is applying for the job.

When it comes to presentation, I don't think you can try hard enough. I would spend far more time than most people would imagine on that aspect.

Image is a vital part of any business. When I came up with the name for Hamilton Bradshaw, my thought process was quite deliberate. I was setting up a private equity firm. I wanted it to sound, from day one, as if it was an old, established business that had been around for ever. I needed it to project a sense of integrity because it would be dealing with money, with investments. I was looking for a name that conjured up all of those things. And for some strange reason – I don't know why – I had an image of the old advert for Bradford & Bingley with the two gents in bowler hats. But in my mind I would not have called them Mr Bradford & Mr Bingley. I would have called them Mr Hamilton & Mr Bradshaw ... So, you can see how much image matters to me. Hamilton Bradshaw depicts or reflects, in my mind, exactly what the company does.

Looking the part

If I was preparing to attend an interview, I would go straight back to the website for the company concerned – having already gutted it for all the information I could find on what the business does. Every company site has a section about their team. I would scroll through the photos of the key staff members and look at what they are wearing in what are likely to have been quite carefully selected images. That exercise, as part of your overall research and preparation, will tell you a lot about what you should be wearing for the interview.

The key, for me, is to be within the range of their look – few companies have a dress code as such, but they do have a distinctive look. Every company has a look. When you walk into any organization, you can tell what that look is. IBM has a look, Nokia and T-Mobile will have a look, Google definitely has a look. As soon as you arrive at Google's offices, you are aware that the atmosphere is very casual, very relaxed. If I walked into Google wearing a blue pinstripe suit, white shirt and red tie I would look wrong.

A company's look also works in reverse. In the mindset of an employer, if you have ever hired somebody from a particular organization and that hiring decision has worked out well, it creates a kind of template, so that if you see somebody else from that type of organization, your mind is already predisposed to give the new candidate the benefit of that positive image.

> ### The JC twist
>
> Although a suit, your smartest suit – don't stint – is always going to be the safest option, and will immediately convey the message that you take care with the impression you make, if you are going for an interview with a company who pride themselves on their maverick, casual approach, do soften the look. I once heard that wearing a three-piece suit if you worked at Virgin was virtually a sacking offence!

Adjust your look according to the message you pick up from the website. Just as you could look too formal in one setting, you might look overly fashionable in another. Both would send out the wrong message. Without sitting on the fence too much, I would suggest that in interviews you aim at the middle. You shouldn't be *over*dressed, because you look like you're trying too hard. You shouldn't be *under*dressed because it gives the impression that you couldn't be bothered to make an effort. It is a difficult balance to get right.

In the good old, bad old days, this was never an issue: a business suit for men and women was the order of the day. As a man all you really needed to think about was the colour of your tie. But as attitudes to work clothes have relaxed and now differ between industry sectors – and between different countries – that decision about what to wear has been made significantly more complex.

I also know this is a controversial point. You can argue all day long about whether your appearance should make a difference, whether in fact the interview should be all about you as a professional, focusing solely on your experience and whether or not you can do the job. The problem is that as an interviewer I am going to see ten or fifteen people and, in the process of elimination, most of the decisions I make are unconscious. I know that I have to make a decision and after the interview, once you have walked out of the door, it is always the things that were *wrong* that stand out. As I am reflecting on the range of candidates I have seen, I will unfortunately remember the guy with the crumpled and frayed suit, and think to myself, 'Mmm, he's not our kind of guy.' I'm not expecting him to have kitted himself out with a bespoke suit from Savile Row's finest, but to have nipped into somewhere like Marks and Spencer and picked up one of their relatively inexpensive but good-looking suits – that's all.

It is important to understand not just the look of the organization but the nature of the job you are applying for. If you walk in for a job that is going to pay £30,000 a year, and there you are sporting a Patek Philippe watch or carrying five grand's worth of handbag and jewellery, I will automatically be thinking, 'This feels wrong.' Trained interviewers will pick those things up.

Rightly or wrongly, we have a perception of people in certain positions. I always have an image of a male investment manager: he is not fashionable, he is not casual, he is supposed to be taken seriously. I don't expect to see an investment manager wearing a casual button-down shirt. If he is not what a client thinks he should be, he has to work that little bit harder to gain their trust. The reality is that we always have some kind of image in our head.

We were hiring an investment manager at Hamilton Bradshaw, and we met one candidate who we really liked at the first interview. When he came back for the second interview, he wasn't wearing a tie and didn't have a jacket on. I was quite surprised. It was not what I was expecting and left me with a mixed message.

Nevertheless, we still called him back for a final interview, so he had the perfect opportunity to redeem himself, but again I was a bit disappointed. For the third interview he was wearing a suit, but still no tie, and – to be honest – the suit he had on looked like it could have done with at least a brief encounter with an iron. The candidate was actually quite good, but everything about his image was wrong.

I was thinking less about his impact on me, more about the impression he would make on clients. He would be interacting with our investee companies, and we are supposed to be seen as the gurus, the experts, the specialists. So I asked him, 'Do you think impressions matter? What do you think the image should be for an investment manager working for Hamilton Bradshaw?' I was hovering around the subject, and in his answers he said all the right things. And yet he didn't look the part. He clearly knew what I was asking, but I don't think he realized that he was not matching the message. Knowing the answers is one thing, delivering them is another.

Attending to the details

When I was just starting out, I went on a sales course that included a session on personal appearance. One of the things the course leader told us was that with men you can tell a lot by the condition of their shoes.

My immediate reaction was, 'That's ridiculous!'

He went on to say, 'Looking after your shoes represents attention to detail. Some people will just get up in the morning, put their shoes on, and they're out of the door. Other people will not leave the house unless their shoes are polished. It's the way they are, it is a characteristic element of their personality. If you are looking for somebody who is articulate, well groomed, takes pride in what they do, has a high level of attention to detail, their shoes are a great indicator that they really are like that.'

Even though the sales course was over twenty-five years ago, the course leader's words have stuck in my head. I still follow his advice to this day. Whenever I am interviewing somebody, either when they walk in or as they leave, I always clock their shoes. And nine times out of ten it works – it tells me something significant about how they see themselves.

Because there is only a short period in which to make a decision, all interviewers have their own individual little quirks. Some people are equally finicky about fingernails – again, it says, 'If you make that level of effort in your personal grooming, that level of attention to detail will be an integral part of your approach to the work that you do.'

The day before the interview, take a moment to pause and

think about what you are going to wear the next day: consider the colour, the style, the look. There are books with plenty of detail on what to wear – I am no Gok Wan, Trinny or Susannah – but the final decision will be down to you.

You would be shocked at the level of detail that I would go into – down to checking your fingernails, looking at your haircut, as a man looking at how you shave, the colour of your shirt, the colour of your tie. When a politician makes an important speech, he and his staff will always make a decision about the colour of his tie. They know it will send out a message – or, more significantly, they know that the wrong tie could send out a damaging message. Why is that different from a job interview? It is exactly the same.

Take care to choose the right briefcase or bag to take to the interview. Whatever you do, don't forget the obvious items such as body odour and fresh breath in the rush to get ready. Now that workplaces are generally no-smoking zones, having a last-gasp cigarette to calm your nerves on top of a cup of coffee might just be a terrible idea.

I would argue, with any interview, 'How do you know this is not going to be the interview that will transform your life?' The answer is: you don't know that. So, why take the risk? Why would you not ensure that, the night before the interview, you think carefully about the shoes, the shirt, the tie, even some-thing as apparently unimportant as your choice of socks? If you turn up in a black suit and you're wearing white socks, it's not good.

When we were hiring a receptionist for Hamilton Bradshaw,

a candidate walked in who was beautifully dressed and immaculately groomed – the perfect look. During the interview she questioned the very job title of 'Receptionist'.

She said, 'I wouldn't call the position "Receptionist". I think it devalues the role.'

'Really,' I said, 'that's interesting. What *would* you call it?'

She replied, 'I would call it Director of First Impressions!'

Of course, I had to smile.

'Because,' she went on, 'that is exactly who I am. I am the first person somebody meets. I firmly believe that when people come into the office, they sit in reception for five or ten minutes, sometimes longer, and my interaction with them is what sets the tone for their perception of Hamilton Bradshaw.'

I looked at her and thought, 'She's absolutely right.'

If I was walking into Hamilton Bradshaw, she is what I would expect to see. The right tone, the right level of friendliness. Companies spend so much money on getting their branding right, on marketing themselves, on the look of their website, all to create a consistent impression. And yet when that is put to the test, when somebody walks through the front door of the building, the look and feel of the reception may be completely at odds. I gave her the job. And when she asked for some business cards, we happily printed them up to say 'Director of First Impressions'.

Fitting in

Another message you have to consider is whether you are suggesting to the interviewer that you are somebody who prefers to work on their own or someone who works well in a team environment. Anyone sitting in the interviewing chair is unconsciously trying to work out, 'Will this person fit in?' The question for you is, **'How can you demonstrate that you will fit into the company?'**

That is something you may have to convey yourself, because it is a question that does not always come up in an interview. Put yourself in the other person's position. In their head he or she will be asking themselves, 'When I put this person into this department, will they fit in?' But they may never articulate that to you. So, your job is to work towards a specific objective in that interview, to deal with the following points:

- Have I done my research?
- Do I know enough about this company?
- Can I demonstrate my ability to do my work?
- Do I look the part?
- What have I done that demonstrates I am competent for the job?

There is an art to conveying that you are a person who can fit in. Over the past few years I have been interviewed many times by journalists, and I consistently use exactly the same techniques. I have learned that whenever the press are doing any kind of interview, they are looking for drama, they want a story. If you are not experienced in dealing with the press, your view is, 'Great, they are coming to interview me because I'm such a great guy, I've done really well and they want to write about this amazing person.' That is the last thing a journalist is there to do. They are not there to promote you, they are there to sell papers.

So you have to learn how to present yourself as an honest, reasonable, fair person and to use your body language and your facial expressions to convey your warmth. It is a matter of psychology and human nature. If you are pleasant to somebody, it is quite difficult for them to go away and attack you in an article. It is exactly the technique you would use if you were being interviewed for a job: you want that person to like you, so whatever you say, how you say it, how you behave, how you act, is all about trying to be accepted by the other person.

Going the extra mile

As you prepare for the interview you could consider what you might take along to the interview to enhance your presentation. These could be credentials, your certificates, your awards, reference letters. Something I generally like to see are examples of your work.

At an interview for one of the investment managers that we hired, he showed me a due diligence report that he had written, and I was really impressed with it. I was trying to evaluate the usual questions: is he right, is he wrong, can he do the job, can't he do the job? There were a hundred things going on in my mind, but that one document answered a lot of my questions.

It demonstrated, in one hit, content, style and information, as well as computer literacy skills from the diagrams and charts integrated into the document. I could gather a large amount of information from that one report very quickly. I didn't sit there reading the whole thing, but I scanned through it. I picked up his writing style. I looked at some of the words he'd used.

For any job there are certain requirements, certain aspects which you can demonstrate in an interview by bringing along a document that proves how you handle them in practice. Within the interview, showing the interviewer that document may be only a two- or three-minute event, but I think in the overall impression you leave it is important.

Mastering the art

Much of what I understand about presentation I learned from one of my first bosses, Tom O'Dwyer. At the time I met Tom, I thought that recruitment and interviewing was a process, like filling out an expenses claim or an application form.

I joined Tom's firm, a financial services company, as a recruitment manager – Tom was one of the directors and owners. When I arrived, the company was getting ready to move to different premises, but was still waiting for the building work to be done. They didn't have an office or a desk for me to use, so Tom said, 'Why don't you share *my* office?' There I was, sharing an office with the director and owner – quite an unbelievable situation for someone in my position.

The company was going through huge growth at the time, and Tom would do all the second and final interviews for the people they were hiring. I watched him run those interviews. It made me realize that this was not a process, but a skill – an art – and Tom was a master at it.

I watched how he phrased questions, the tone of his voice, the actions that he used, his body language. I was in awe of how somebody had taken the process to such a level of skill. And his strike rate was phenomenal. Ninety-five per cent of all the candidates Tom interviewed wanted the job – because it's a two-way process. The employer should be selling the job opportunity to you just as much as you will be selling yourself to them.

If somebody mentioned to Tom that someone who worked at Allied Dunbar had just won a contract with BA, Tom wouldn't even hesitate. He was completely fearless, would pick up the phone straight away, call the guy, pitch the job to him on the phone, get him in, and then it was like flicking a switch: off he went. He was brilliant. The way he dressed was never too flamboyant, never too dull, always crisp white shirts. It was not fashionable, but it was impeccably smart. He would never drink out of a mug, he would only drink out of a cup and saucer, because he thought it was more elegant. He was very expressive with his hands when he spoke. He thought about the angle at which he positioned himself, and where the candidate sat. Over time I asked him questions about almost every aspect of the process. As my desk was behind the candidate they could not see me, but I had a ringside seat.

When the candidate had left, I would ask, because I am

naturally curious, 'Tom, when you asked him that question, why did you get up?'

He'd say, 'Because I could see the guy was very nervous, and I wanted to put him at his ease.'

He had the skill to read body language so well, to think to himself that because he had clearly asked a question which had made the candidate uncomfortable, he should make a small gesture to defuse the situation. I have applied that sense of presentation and thought during interviews ever since.

One of the best interviews I have ever given was when I was approached by the head of a private equity company in America who wanted to buy my recruitment business. Now, when you're selling a recruitment company, it's a people business. The people who run that business *are* the business. You are not buying the furniture or the leases. The value of the business is in the goodwill, and the goodwill in this instance was me.

The guy called me, and said, 'I've heard so much about your company. I really want to fly over from the States and meet you.'

As he was on his way I was thinking to myself, 'If I present myself and the company in a light that is not engaging, he is not going to make me an offer.'

I remember waking up on the morning of the meeting feeling really nervous. In a way I was getting myself ready for an interview. Most people would never have thought about it in those terms. They would have considered it a straight financial presentation. 'Here's somebody who's interested in buying the company, so let me bring in the chief accountant and we'll sit down together and run through the figures.' But I looked at it in reverse, and thought that if I was buying somebody's business and it was purely a people business, the numbers were secondary. I was the founder of the company, I had built the company and I was the chief executive. In his place I would be thinking, 'If I don't believe that James is the right guy, that I can work with him, that I can interact with him, if I don't buy into his vision, his integrity and his professionalism, why would I buy his business? Because I am buying his business in order for him to continue to run it.'

I remember feeling exactly as I'd done before job interviews. Did I get up that morning and make sure my shoes were polished? Absolutely right, I did. Was my shirt crisp, white and

---

The JC twist

Whether you are going for a regular business meeting, or giving a press interview, or attending a job interview, the approach is the same. What's the difference between an interview and a first date? Aren't you there on a first date to sell yourself? If you are getting ready to go on a first date, what is the mental preparation you do? It's exactly the same. When you open the wardrobe, do you just throw anything on? Never. You are very particular about which shirt you are going to wear, which shoes you are going to choose, how your hair looks. Even if you're a guy you are going to check in the mirror three times before you leave the house. In every meeting, every interaction that you have, the way you decide to put yourself on display is sending out a message.

ironed? Yes, it was. Did I pick out the right suit? Of course. It wasn't a dramatic pinstripe suit, it was a plain navy suit, with a white shirt, red tie. It had to be clean, professional; I needed to present a solid image.

Before each and every interview you need to go through a detailed mental checklist. If I was alongside you, taking you through every step, I would insist that you put a tick against every box, double-checking every single aspect. Is your shirt unironed? Bad sign – it looks terrible. Have you thought about your tie, your hair? I would question you about everything – down to your nails, the pen you are taking along, the pad you're going to use for note-taking, the way you sit, the way you shake the interviewer's hand, the way you acknowledge questions.

Think about how you will interact throughout the process.

- Have you addressed the list of questions that you are going to be asking?
- Have you prepared and considered all the information that you have researched about the company?
- Have you thought through the highlights of the job that you are applying for so that you can make sure you have addressed each of the elements?

At each stage I would ask, **What is the point in gambling that you might get it wrong?**

All of this is what it takes to get the job that is going to transform your life.

"As a result of the candidate-saturated market, employers' expectations are at an all-time high, so you're going to have to pull off a fantastic performance."

6. PERFORMANCE

It is the day of the interview. How confident are you feeling?

Confidence at an interview comes from knowledge. If you have not done your research, if you haven't studied the company, if you haven't gone on the Web, if you haven't understood what the market is and who the competition is, if you haven't done a Google search on the person who's interviewing you, your confidence is going to be very low. Conversely, the more knowledgeable you are, the more thoroughly you have done your research, the more confident you will feel.

If you have followed the ideas in the previous chapters, your confidence should be at an all-time high. You have finished and reviewed your detailed research about the company you are going to see. You have thought about the way you are going to present yourself. You have taken time to reflect on the key messages you want to get across during the interview, and on how those messages match the job specification and what you believe to be your potential employer's expectations.

Now it's show time. Think of your job interview as putting on the best performance of your life. This chapter is all about giving yourself that extra 'X' factor.

Remembering the simple things

Many of the basics of performing well in a job interview, just like the way you present yourself, should really be second nature, pure common sense – and yet, *and yet*, people still forget them.

These basics start well before you arrive at the interview venue. The simple things to remember include getting a good sleep the night before – it's not a good evening to go out on the town and stay out late. Obvious, you'd think. Don't believe it!

Punctuality is key – give yourself a reasonable amount of leeway to take account of the usual hassles in getting to any meeting: traffic jams, delayed trains, complicated directions. Make sure you are in the neighbourhood of the interview venue good and early so that you are not dashing in at the last moment drenched in sweat. Allow yourself enough time to collect your thoughts – maybe have a juice at a café round the corner – and relax as best you can before going into the reception area on time.

Turning up in good time and wearing a clean, smart outfit is only half the battle. What really matters is how you project yourself and how you engage with the interviewer or interviewers. So, when I say you need to give the performance of your life, I mean in the context of giving a job interview, and getting the job.

The interview represents a completely different phase of the job process, for both sides. The interview takes us back to basics again. As an interviewer, I have already whittled the applicants down, and in my mind there is a certain hierarchy based on the information I have picked up from the CVs. But more often than not experience tells me the candidate who on paper looks as if they are going to be really good generally is not. There is only so much you can pick up from a piece of paper, or even a video clip.

You can take confidence from this thought: there may be people who are a hundred times better qualified than you – with better experience, better grades – who tick every box. But if they walk through the door and are as dull as dishwater, they are not going to get the job. You can be average, even mediocre, in content and experience – you could almost have *no* experience – but still convince the interviewer and get the job. It's about how you present yourself, about your communication skills. If I listed the things that stood out about every person I have ever hired, personality and the ability to communicate would rank the highest.

It starts as soon as you walk into the interview. Be aware of your body language. If you walk in and you are slouching, or your hands are sweating – that's not great. When you shake my hand, if it's a weak and woolly grip, before you've even opened your mouth I have formed an opinion. We have made contact, and that contact is more important than you think.

As human beings, the minute we make contact, there is an instant reaction. Something happens: it creates an impression. If you come in, say confidently, 'Nice to meet you, James,' extend your hand, grip mine with a dry, firm, solid handshake, look me straight in the eye, I can't help it: as a human being, I pick up a positive, professional message. You are in control already.

I don't want wet and woolly, but equally I don't want to be on the end of the bone-crusher handshake – both extremes will send me a negative message. I've already got the wrong impression. My mind is telling me something, and you will have to work harder to climb back up in my estimation again.

Breaking the ice

Before the interview gets into full swing, and you find yourself trapped on the wrong end of a Q&A session, try and find something that allows you to connect with the interviewer on a personal level. As you come into their office, out of the corner of your eye you might see a photograph – of their family, their kids, some event, maybe a shot of them crossing the finishing line of the London Marathon or the Great North Run. There's your cue. 'Oh, when did you take part in the marathon? I'm thinking of going in for it next year' – who's going to know whether that's true or not! 'Was the training worse than you thought? What charity were you running to raise money for?'

In many of the companies I visit, I see an award has been put up on the wall of an office: there's another prompt just waiting for you to pick up on. 'I notice you won Best Newcomer in Pharmaceuticals last year; that was an interesting achievement. Who were you up against?' And the minute you ask that question about a time when they had some glory, they of course sit up with a big smile. You're talking about their success, which is difficult to do with a glum face, and the conversation is under way in a very positive vein. You are engaged in a dialogue already.

Even if the interview is taking place in a rather sterile meeting room – as it often does these days – you can pick up on something you spotted while you were sitting in the reception area, where the same kind of certificates and awards might be on display. 'While I was waiting in reception, I saw you guys have picked up a Product of the Year award: which product was that for?'

Minimizing the surprise factor

Unlike your CV – the creation of which is completely under your control – each interview is something of an unknown quantity. But you can do plenty to minimize being thrown off your stride. The best interview is going to be the one which contains the fewest surprises – no hidden traps – because you have thought through the process in advance. And you have taken the trouble to get to know the job you are applying for. Nine out of ten people have a very superficial idea of the job itself. They might know the basic details from the job ad – Marketing

Manager, £30,000 a year salary, five years' experience, must have graphic skills – but beyond that they are essentially trying to wing it.

On the day of an interview, the desire to get the job and a natural adrenalin rush – a positive nervousness – tend to make you focus on yourself. You are checking everything *you* need is in place, thinking about the logistics of how *you* will get there, running through what *you* want to say. There will be a lot going on in the interview, many different elements to keep in mind, a flexible attitude to maintain.

As soon as you can – as soon as you dare – stop thinking about yourself and put yourself in the mind of the interviewer, who will be looking at you and listening to you. He or she is the person who is going to put you through to the next round of interviews, or make the hiring decision there and then. Ask yourself, **What will be happening in the interviewer's brain?**

As an interviewer, every interview is in essence a subconscious checklist. All the way through the conversation, you are ticking boxes in your head, often without even realizing it. And as the candidate says goodbye and thanks, you have already mentally scored the individual.

Many interviewers will actually write down a score as the candidate leaves the room. I do it too: I jot down an A, B or C, or I write down a number: 7, 8, 9 – I never give a 10. If the score is below 7, I don't bother, because that person is not going to get a second interview. A 7 means I am at least going to bear them in mind, although I am clearly not sure. And along with that grade

I will jot down a comment – a trigger – something to remind me of that candidate and the conversation we had when I come to assess all the candidates I have seen.

If you, the interviewee, know what the interviewer's checklist consists of, and what they are trying to achieve, once you understand that, your ability to get the job has just gone up by seventy per cent because you know exactly what you should be focusing on. How many people actually do that? My gut feeling is less than twenty per cent.

In the interview process, if you are able to maintain control of the interview, the chances are you will get the job. Most people think that taking control might be too arrogant, that it might intimidate the interviewer or prove a turn-off for the potential employer – absolutely not in my opinion.

The way to do this without intimidating the interviewer is by getting in with an early question after the initial small talk, and before anything can slip away from you: 'I understand the position is for a marketing manager. It sounds really exciting. Could I ask you a question, James – what are the five key components of this job that are really important to this organization?'

The interviewer will be obliged to give you an answer. 'Well, in this particular role, we've got a major client, Shell, so we need somebody who understands that sector, but who can bring in the relevant creativity and design skills, and is able to run a team of six people.'

In answer to your question they have told you exactly what they want from the job and what you want to know.

You can go on to ask, 'Could you tell me a bit about the person who is in the role at the moment, or who last performed the job?'

Just by the interviewer's reply, 'Oh, it was a he or a she and they were in their mid-thirties,' you now know something useful.

Your response might be, 'And what were the things they did that really impressed you?'

Once the interviewer has laid it out on a plate for you, all you have to do is match your skills against their wish list. By all means make notes, because he or she is giving you the five key components of the job, and your task is now to demonstrate that you are competent in each of those areas. As you do so, subconsciously the interviewer will be sitting there ticking off those five critical components, thinking, 'Oh, that's quite interesting, she can do this, she can do that.' It will then be very difficult for them to say afterwards that you are not right for the job. Whenever you are able to, bring that question into play as early as you can. If you leave it too long you might have talked yourself out of the job by focusing on the wrong issues.

When I attend business meetings that are not interviews, I use exactly the same technique. I arrive at the meeting and say, 'Firstly, thank you for taking the time to see me. Can I ask you a question: what are the three things you would like to achieve from this meeting?' The minute they tell me that, I can see the entire landscape of their agenda and pick out the right path to get to where I want to be.

Again, the whole skill lies in knowing the questions you should be asking.

Making your body language work for you

Here is something to try and consider, even in the pressurized setting of an interview: your facial expressions throughout the meeting are really important. When asking a question, most people are quite serious. If you are asking questions with a smile, it is very warm, very interactive. There is nothing worse than sitting there looking very serious, very intense.

While I am interviewing you and engaged in the conversation, remember that I am subconsciously scoring you. One of the key issues for me is whether you will fit in. People who are relaxed, warm, friendly, and who smile are much easier to fit into an organization than somebody who is a bit tense, who lacks personality and looks like he or she won't be able to integrate.

Controlling facial expressions was something I learned from sitting in Tom O'Dwyer's office. I noticed that in one particular interview, every time he asked a difficult question he smiled: he was self-aware enough to do that deliberately. He was asking a tough, negative question that he knew the candidate would struggle to answer – 'You said in the last three years you achieved *x*, but in fact that last year was a terrible year, wasn't it? Your numbers weren't great. So, tell me, what actually happened?' – but he was asking it in such a manner that it allowed the candidate to engage with him in a more positive way.

Self-awareness is the key. You can study in great detail the art of body language, of mirroring techniques, of neurolinguistic programming – you can probably get a degree in it now – but in reality the basics are not rocket science. Make sure your body language matches the message you are sending out verbally. Don't fiddle, tap your nails on the desk, or grip your legs as if you are holding on for dear life. And don't concentrate so hard on what you are doing with your hands that you forget to listen to what the interviewer has just asked you.

This is where your performance skills have to come into play. The knack is to perform well while appearing to be natural. You should, of course, try not to be a bag of nerves because the interviewer needs to feel confidence in you in order to feel comfortable with you. But if you do show some nerves, that is fine, because nerves are natural – and they show you really want this job. If you do make a slip in something you say, simply apologize straight away and then say what you intended to. Natural reactions are the key: being overly cocky and giving too slick a performance can send out the message that you're not a very good team player.

Using humour to gain an advantage

Humour is a great relaxer, though potentially a minefield. However, in any business meeting I am involved in, I will always aim to get one laugh, or at the very least raise a warm smile. It forms part of my own mental checklist. Whether the moment comes right at the beginning of the meeting, or later on, some-where I try and find a little one-liner that clicks.

When I am interviewing someone, there's a little comment I usually like to throw in when I am asking a question about which qualities their current boss would describe as their strongest. They usually come up with something quite earnest along the lines of, 'Well, I think she would probably say that I am a strong team player, and that the kind of solutions I come up with are creative but also very practical.'

As I'm wrapping up the question, I say, as casually as possible, 'Now would you like to know what she *really* said?'

The candidate always freezes in panic . . . But I don't let them suffer too long. 'I'm only kidding.' They are so relieved to find out I was actually winding them up that they always laugh and relax.

If you cannot introduce an element of humour into a 45-minute interview, that will score against you. You don't have to be a stand-up comedian. Far from it – you should retain a gentle sense of humour, but avoid pre-prepared jokes. The line you use to create a smile does not have to be about anything specific. It is a question of spotting a moment in the conversation where a slice of self-deprecation or a neatly judged observation will come naturally. Humour that works relaxes the environment; it sets a tone.

This is a judgement call that will be down to you. You cannot use humour more than once – twice at a pinch – because then there is a danger I won't take you seriously. Three times certainly goes completely against you. I have turned people down

Cockiness can be a dangerous ploy. But if, like me, you have a natural cheek, you can use that – at the right time. In one of my very first interviews, aged seventeen or so, I was applying for a job in the accounts department of Grand Metropolitan. I had made up my mind to show the woman interviewing me that I could do the job – one I was not qualified for on paper. In fact I had virtually no relevant experience.

In the middle of the interview she asked me, 'Are you very numerate?'

'Well, reasonably numerate . . .'

She came back with, 'OK, what's 13 x 83?'

I did some quick mental maths, and came up with the correct answer.

She smiled and said, 'That's really good.'

So, I said, 'Can I ask *you* a question?'

'Sure.'

'What's 19 x 34?'

We both smiled. And she got it wrong!

She asked me if I knew the answer.

I said, 'I think so' and calculated it in my head, while she had to check it on her calculator.

She was still smiling. The rest of the interview was a breeze, and I got the job.

because, although I have thought, 'He's a really nice guy,' there have been a few too many jokes.

Engaging your audience

You don't have to be a Barack Obama of oratory. Simply imagine you are giving a one-man or one-woman show, and engage your audience in the conversation. Draw them into what you are saying by explaining the value you have brought to other companies through specific achievements, but tell them as stories, not as a series of boasts.

Even though you have done a lot of detailed research – and as I've said, I really don't mind if you refer to your notes in the interview – if you can speak naturally from that information, so much the better. When I give a speech now, I try if at all possible never to use notes or cards. Although I will have read my notes beforehand, I try to think through and position the speech in my head, not on paper. When I arrive onstage, I will follow the structure in my head, using key words to focus on. The delivery is all-important: content which scores 6 out of 10 and delivery which scores 9 works a lot better than 9 for content and 6 for delivery.

I had to learn this the hard way. When I was first invited to give a speech, I had written everything down. I stood up and read off my cards.

Later I asked somebody I knew in the audience, 'What did you think?'

He said, 'I thought it was useless.'

'It's OK,' I dead-panned, 'you can be straight with me, I can take it. Was it really that good?'

'James, it was boring.'

'Really, why?'

'Because you didn't once look at the audience, you read off your notes. It was monotonous. It was stale.'

He absolutely destroyed my presentation. Which was great – thank goodness he did.

At the same event I watched another speaker, and he was brilliant. He moved around, he used his arms, he worked with the crowd, he didn't have any notes. I engaged with him. The interesting thing was, if you'd asked me afterwards what he had actually said, there was nothing compelling, but I *enjoyed* the speech. I spoke to the event manager, asked him to send me a copy of the event video, and set about improving my technique.

Prepare, rehearse, have a mental structure, and deliver what you want to say in your own style. Focus, of course, but don't prepare to the extent where you lose your individuality. Whenever I am delivering a speech, I am projecting my personality, my style. The content is not the key. With a joke, it's not the quality of the joke, it's the quality of the delivery that makes you laugh. We all know that from when we've tried retelling a joke we heard on TV and it falls completely flat – the words are the same but, to coin a phrase, 'It's the way you tell 'em.'

Investing in your own success

What better material to pitch in a natural way than something
you have already prepared? I always expect that there will be
candidates who turn up with nothing – those people who have
not even bothered checking out the website. But there have been
a number of people who have arrived with a full-blown presentation, a document of six to ten pages, and said, 'James, I've been
thinking about this opportunity, and about Hamilton Bradshaw.'
They have gone into a presentation about the company, its
history, who the competition is, who we're comparable with,
a selection of interesting data on any of the investments we've
made, and ended with how their experience could fit. I sit there
and think, 'Wow!' I am not saying that if you do that, it will
guarantee you get the job, but it certainly adds that wow factor,
because it shows exactly how serious you are about the job
on offer.

In my mind, you have a limited window of opportunity to
win points on my mental scorecard. With a strong presentation
you certainly cannot lose points, you can only gain them. A pitch
document also expresses your style, your thought processes,
the quality of your content. It tells me a lot about somebody,
especially in a work sense. Doing that research is important, and
the beauty is that frankly it is so easy to do. Google will provide
you with everything you want on the organization, the people,
the market, the product, the competition. Everything is available
to you, and how long will it take you to collate that information?

The answer is: half a day, tops. You only need to invest half a day of effort.

> ### The JC twist
>
> If I was going to an interview and had spent time creating a knock-out presentation, I would completely undersell it. The way I would describe the presentation is, 'I don't know if this is useful, but I've put down a few ideas on paper.' I would be giving the interviewer an amazing document but presenting it as something that I had jotted down, because I don't want them to think I've made a huge effort. It's a bit like going on a date. You don't want to let your date know you've spent four hours getting dressed. You want to give the impression that you just threw something on. While you are talking through the presentation the interviewer will be sitting there flicking through the pages, picking up on the style, the content, the quality, the research, the writing. And thinking, 'If this is something they've just jotted down, I'd love to see what they think of as a real presentation.'

Because of my involvement with *Dragons' Den*, I had to hire a communications manager: the profile the programme has given me meant I was doing more and more work with the press and media. It was becoming ridiculous: every day somebody was ringing up, asking, 'Will you come on CNBC or CNN or the BBC?'

My PA said to me, quite rightly, 'James, this is not a job for me. I can take the messages but I can't talk to these people, I don't know what they are looking for, how to choose between them.'

I said, 'OK, let's hire a communications manager.'

One of the candidates who came in had put together a pitch document about how he would represent me in the media and in the press, what my style should be, what my voice should be, the topics I should speak about, the topics that I should steer clear of. In this document he had included a number of press articles that had been written about me in a section called 'The Dos and the Don'ts' in which he said, 'I would have done this article, but not that one. This one conveys the right things, but this one dilutes your message – a lot of the information is inconsistent'. He was taking a bit of a flyer by being quite up front about it.

He had also been very critical about the company website. He had studied it in real detail, identifying the elements he really liked, those sections that he felt did not work. If I had to be honest, we almost offered him the position on the back of the document. The document spelled the job out better than we had; singlehandedly he had crystallized what the job was. We had not really worked out the spec, because we had never needed to hire anyone like that – I had never been in this position before. I would say our job description scored 4 out of 10, and his document scored an impressive 8 out of 10.

Being prepared to adapt

As the interview progresses, listen to what the interviewer is saying and the signals they are giving out. Like any great entertainer you need to sense the mood in the room. The direction and the wording of their questions will usually indicate whether they want you to give more detail or less, whether they want to hear more about your past experience or about your future ambitions.

Use your 'antennae' to judge how things are going. Sometimes you can tell from the interviewer's body language alone. You should be very observant as a candidate, looking for those signs, seeing how your pitch is going, whether the interviewer is accepting what you are saying. If the interviewer is getting distracted, losing focus, you know you're not doing very well. If the atmosphere is ultra-friendly, positive, then clearly the way you are approaching the interview, your whole style, is working. If you can read that, then you know how to play the remainder of the interview. If you are not getting those vibes, you know you've got to change tack. And if you are not sure, you can always throw in a question to gauge the interviewer's reaction.

Sometimes the person interviewing you actually says, 'You're the best candidate I've seen.' This isn't something the interviewer should say if they want the candidate to work hard for the job. That kind of remark doesn't help anybody, because then the candidate takes it for granted that the job is theirs, which is not good. Remember, we always want to join the club we can't get into.

You will know when you haven't performed well after the interview. That is the time to be self-critical, self-analytical. Ask yourself: 'Where did I go wrong? What do I need to work on?'

And never forgetting ...

Finally, remember the closing question you know will be asked:
'Have you got any questions?'

I always, always ask that question towards the end of the interview. So do the vast majority of employers. Seventy per cent of candidates are either going to say, 'No, I'm fine, thank you,' or come up with a couple of very woolly questions because they have not done their research thoroughly enough. On a scale of 1 to 10, I would say the average question I get asked scores no more than a 5.

If you say, 'Actually, there *are* a couple of questions, James, if you have two minutes. Recently you launched this new product, how's it going?' immediately I'm impressed – a) how did you know? and b) I have to justify the answer to you.

'Well, we launched it three months ago, but it hasn't done as well as we hoped yet,' or whatever the case is.

At that point the quality of your question has a bigger impact than you might think on my decision to hire you or not. The way you decide to respond tells me a lot about you. You know I am going to ask you – so make sure you have something ready to fire back at me.

I hope by now you have realized that so much of success in getting a job is down to preparation and rehearsal. So, when you step through that door and on to the interview 'stage', I want you to be in as good a shape as you'll ever be.

Go on, knock 'em dead.

'There is always an element of cat and mouse in any interview situation, so make sure you don't end up as the cat's next meal. Come away with the interviewer thinking you're top dog instead.'

7. POWER

Once you are in the interview, you may find your interviewer is enjoying the sense of power that they automatically gain by being in charge of selecting who is going to get the job on offer. They will try and push you off balance to make sure that their power is unchallenged. Your mission, should you decide to accept it, is to know and understand the logic behind the usual tricks of the trade – and believe me, most of them are as old as the hills – and turn them to your own benefit.

Some of these tricks are quite predictable. The interviewer might choose to sit in an executive chair behind his or her desk. You, the interviewee, end up having to squat awkwardly on a low, soft chair. It's not very subtle.

The first, and most important, response is not to let something so blatant get to you. Then try and come up with a displacement activity. If there is a meeting table in the office, ask if you can both sit there so you can get your paperwork or presentation out – even if that's just your CV.

Although I think you can overplay the furniture angle, the one thing that I always do in this setting is move my chair closer, even if it's only very slightly, towards the other person. It is a small gesture but I think it speaks volumes. It demonstrates that I am very confident in myself and that I am happy to be closer to you. It indicates that I am taking control.

Sometimes I will walk into one of those classic boardrooms and find a table for ten people, with four chairs on two sides, and one at either end. The interviewer is usually sitting at one end, in the chairman's seat. What normally happens, simply because of human nature, is that most people choose to sit in the second or third chair away from the interviewer. I would walk straight up to the first chair, right next to them. You might think that is a bit too close for comfort, but I know there is a message there.

The same thing happens when people walk into any kind of conference. There are certain people who naturally gravitate to the back of the hall, others who head for the middle and some who go straight to the front. There are no signs to direct anybody to their seat, but you will see that automatic decision being made every single time. It is important to know which direction you would take instinctively, and if necessary change your natural inclination for the purposes of an interview.

If you know you are deliberately being physically placed in a difficult position, understand that it is nothing more than a ploy – and a rather transparent piece of manipulation – and you will find you can override it.

Asking the right questions

Bear in mind that I have been recruiting and interviewing for a long time. If you are coming for an interview with me, you will always get a very tough interview. Because I have heard *all* the textbook answers, a thousand times over, the objective for me in each interview is to dig and dig and dig, to discover places you have never even thought about and ask questions that will make you completely uncomfortable. I am always aiming to get through the veneer.

Here's a question for you. **How many questions are you going to ask?**

You need to take control. Because if you don't, the interviewer will. And if the interviewer has taken control, it's because you have allowed them to do so. How do you avoid that? You make sure that you ask as many questions as they do.

As a candidate I would always aim to ask fifty per cent of the questions in an interview. Normally the interviewee talks for at least seventy per cent of the time, but if you think about it analytically, that is absolutely wrong, because both you and the interviewer are there for the same reason.

You need to know whether this job is right for you: is the company right for you, can you do the job, do you want the job? You are in exactly the same position as the employer, who needs to know the answers to precisely those same questions. That's why it has to be 50/50. When you walk out of the door, if you want to know how well you have performed, ask yourself how much interaction took place. If the interviewer asked fifteen questions to your five, it probably went against you. In order for the interview to go well, you have to match him blow for blow, question for question.

Take every chance to drill down into the role itself and challenge the interviewer about the components of the job. Generic questions such as, 'What are the hours?', 'What's the size of the team?' will not tell you anything significant. What you really want to do is ask, 'Tell me a bit about the role: what is a typical day? What am I expected to do? Do I have KPIs? Am I going to be measured? Are there quarterly appraisals? How often will I report to my manager? What is my manager looking for from me?' Give yourself every opportunity to evaluate the job for yourself.

Imagine you're the interviewer. You've had ten interviews – all very standard. Somebody walks in and all of a sudden puts you on the spot, challenges you, asks you a couple of tough questions. *That's* the interview you're going to enjoy.

Does that show overconfidence on the candidate's part? Let me tell you something. At the end of the day, when you reflect back on the ten people you met, the one who will stand out is the person who asked the right questions and who challenged you.

I interviewed somebody quite recently who said, 'James, I was quite interested to read that you'd actually invested in a business that failed.'

That immediately got my back up, and I said, 'Really? Which one was that?' All of a sudden I was engaged, because now he was almost interviewing me. I had to justify the statement he'd made, so I said, 'That's interesting. Where did you read that?'

'On such and such a website.'

Now I had to explain. I had no choice.

With a question like that, the dynamics of human nature mean I have to respond. So, I'm now explaining to you. The balance of power has just shifted away from me, the decision maker, towards you, the candidate.

Fending off the killer questions

All interviewers believe they have at least one killer question up their sleeve that will have you babbling like an idiot. Again, these are very rarely original – but that doesn't mean the question will not generate valuable information for the interviewer.

Early on in my career I learned that you should never answer a difficult question directly. Don't jump straight in with the script you've been rehearsing for days. Wait a moment or two to mull it over in your head. You will sound more coherent and more confident and the interviewer will see that you are giving his or her question the weight it deserves.

The strategies in this chapter will allow you to keep on a level playing field. Although you are trying to gain the upper hand, there is no need to arm-wrestle the interviewer to the ground. As my father taught me from a very early age, the art of success is making the other person feel as if they have won.

Curve-ball questions can catch you out, of course – you can prepare for almost every eventuality, but not every single one. I was appearing on *Question Time* on BBC 1, alongside a sophisticated, informed panel. One of the audience members came up with a question that completely threw me. I very rarely get fazed, but no answer was coming to mind. Usually there is a mental process in which somehow your brain is able to capture an answer of some description. But this time, within seconds, I realized, 'I don't know the answer.' But I knew I had to remain composed, as the cameras were trained on me.

So, I said, 'That's a really good question – but, you know what? I don't know the answer,' and smiled brightly. It got a laugh, and the programme moved on. After the show one of the other panel members came up to me and said, 'By the way, James, that was brilliant.' It was all about confidence. Most people respond to a question they find difficult by fumbling the question, and trying to bluff the answer. The problem is, everyone knows that is what you are doing.

I generally have a couple of standard responses ready for curve-ball questions. First of all, in a business situation, I would say, 'That's a really good question. Do you mind if I get back to you on that?' But it is not the words you use, it is how you deliver them. I acknowledge it was a good question – and always smile – because clearly you've caught me out. I don't want you to feel as though you've won, so I say, 'Great question, can we pick that one up later?' Park it and carry on. By saying, 'Thank you very much, can we come back to that?' I have balanced the position.

My second option with a difficult question is to get a glass of water. I want to buy some time, because there are questions where it would be inappropriate to say, 'Could we come back to that answer?' There are certain situations where you *have* to answer the question. As the process of pouring out the water is going on, my brain is composing the answer.

A lot of people suggest answering a tricky question with another question. That depends on who is interviewing you. If you did that to me, I would bat it right back to you. I would say, 'That's a really good question. Now, can we just go back to my original question?' I would get you straight back. I won't accept a question answered with a question.

As with the 'Have you got any questions?' question, take some time to prepare quick and simple replies to apparently tricky questions in advance. There are a number of angles I use when I am interviewing. One of the ones I particularly like is,

'Give me three reasons why I wouldn't hire you.'

It's a variation on the classic, 'What do you think your weaknesses are?'

And the first response I get is usually, 'I can't think of any.'

'No, no,' I say, 'I need three reasons – give me three reasons.'

I never let them get away with it. I want to hear their three reasons. It tells me a lot about the person, because they have to say something. I make them answer the question. And once I have pushed it, a good debate follows.

Don't roll over and give the interviewer an insight into your insecurities and fallibilities, because that's tantamount to rejecting the job before it's even been offered. Choose a weakness and make sure it is nothing to do with the core elements of the job you are applying for. So, if you're being interviewed for a human resources job, pick a slight weakness in your experience of the financial side of business – but then turn it around, by saying you have asked to be sent on a course to brush up on that.

Here are a couple of other options. You can say, 'I am a bit of a workaholic. I take my work home with me; I don't know when to switch off.' That's a great answer because it is a negative, but it is very well put. Or, 'I have been criticized for being a perfection-ist. Sometimes it's better to get the job done than to be overly focused on the detail, because it means I take a lot longer than other people. I realize that aspect of my work can frustrate my colleagues, but it's just who I am.' Again, as an employer I want to hear that.

The other line of questioning that often catches candidates out is when I say, 'Imagine you are standing in front of a client, a client we have been desperately looking to win for the last year. Unfortunately I have been taken ill and you have to step into my meeting at short notice. You've got two minutes – 120 seconds – to pitch me the company.'

I would say that nearly a third of the people I have asked to pitch back to me have lost the interview on the back of that. They have pitched it really, really poorly. I think there is no excuse for that. And I have closed the interview no more than ten minutes after that, completely switched off, because the pitch was so appalling.

I time the candidate, just for effect. I get out my mobile phone and say, 'I've got a stopwatch here. Are you ready? Go.' Then I sit back and watch. Generally they manage to last no more than thirty seconds before they lose the thread. I don't care whether the job is for an accounts assistant, a PA, a receptionist, or a managerial position. I am not asking you for a two-hour lecture, I'm not asking you for a thousand-word essay. I'm saying two minutes. All I really need is the home page of our website. That's all it is. It is no more than what we say about ourselves. If you can't do that, goodbye.

The twist on that is for me to ask, 'Why on earth would anybody want to work for Hamilton Bradshaw? This is a nightmare. We're frantic, the pressure's crazy.' I usually get a glazed look back, because it's an unexpected question, coming from an employer. Again, if you have not done your homework, you'll fumble. You need to come straight back at me with, 'Yes, but James, Hamilton Bradshaw is a market leader, you've done this, your performance has been that.'

Another question I always ask in every interview, even if I've only interviewed one person, is, 'Just so you understand, I have met six other people for this role. What is it about you that makes you think you stand out among all the other people I have met for this position?' The candidate is forced to declare their strengths. It saves me from working it out. And then I follow that up with the flip side: 'If you were me, give me one reason why I shouldn't offer you this position.' Remember that experienced interviewers will often ask the same question dressed up in a number of different ways.

I will often ask, 'If I called the three referees you have identified, tell me exactly what they would say.' You don't know whether I am going to call them or not, so you can't make it up. If I do call them and hear the opposite to what you tell me, you have just lost the job. That's when I add in the joke about whether you want to know what your boss *really* said . . .

Everyone comes into an interview prepared to answer

questions about their CV. Most interviewers will be happy to take you through what you have already prepared. But what happens sometimes is that even after talking through the CV, I haven't really got *you*. I am trying to work *you* out. So I will say, 'That all sounds interesting, but I need to know who you are – tell me about you. Who are you outside work? Are you married, have you got kids, what are they doing?' Your face will drop, because it's the one aspect you haven't thought about. I have taken you away from your chosen subject. I usually learn quite a lot by asking that question, and by a follow-up, if you have children: 'What career would you like your kids to be in?' If you are really proud of the industry you are part of, I would expect you to want them to follow in the same line of work. If you don't, there is a message there for me. And at the end of the interview, when I am reflecting on the discussion, out of the forty-five minutes, that might be the only thing that sticks in my mind: the fact you aren't that committed to the work you are in.

Over the past few years we have seen refracted through TV a version of what a tough job interview is – either the *Dragons' Den* process or the section of *The Apprentice* where the remaining contestants go up in front of Alan Sugar's hand-picked team of interviewers. That whole process is designed to test the contestants' mettle. It is less about content than about stamina.

Whenever I interviewed sales people, I always used to put them through one particular exercise.

I would give the candidate an ashtray and say, 'Sell me this ashtray.'

They'd come back with, 'But I don't smoke.'

'That's not the point. I want you to sell me the ashtray.'
Whatever they were going to say to me, I was going to give them
a hard time.

They would get into the pitch: 'Hi, I'm from the Diamond
Ashtray Company and, James, I'd like to present this ashtray.'

At this point I'd say, 'I'm sorry, I don't smoke.' Whatever angle
they took, I'd come up with a counter. In a post-smoking-ban
world, I had to come up with a new version – so I might pick up
my mobile phone and say, 'I'm thinking of changing my phone.
Sell me yours,' and whatever feature of their phone they pitch, I'll
say I don't need it.

The objective of the exercise is not to ascertain your technical
knowledge of the ins and outs of ashtrays or mobile phones.
What I am trying to establish is how much grit there is inside you,
how resilient you are, how you respond to rejection. Because if
you are going to join me in sales, how many times do you think
you are going to be rejected? I am putting you on the spot to see
how creatively you can think under pressure. How quickly do you
give up?

I know it sounds crazy, but so many times this exercise made
up my mind. If the candidate did freeze, even though I might have
liked them, even though their CV might have been exceptional,
I would be thinking, 'This is a sales position. In this job they're
going to pick up the phone, or go out and see somebody, and the
potential customer will say, "I'm not interested." If the candidate
has dried up, hasn't even attempted to come back to me, I am not
interested in his background. I don't think he's right for the job.'

Too many people would take the exercise literally. My

recommendation is to be as crazy as you like, because you're not being tested on technical substance. You can make the whole thing up. It doesn't matter. The thrust of the exercise is: how do you think when you are in a sales position? And the whole objective of the exercise is for the candidate to understand what the interviewer is looking for by asking them the right question.

We were interviewing somebody for a financial position, and I asked him as part of the discussion, 'What's 17.5 per cent of 28,500?' He couldn't answer – he just sat there, looking blank. Because he immediately assumed that he was not allowed to use a calculator. Now I hadn't said he couldn't use a calculator. I just asked the question.

He could have asked for a calculator. But that would not have impressed me. What *would* have impressed me was if he'd had the wit to use the calculator on his mobile phone. In the real world, if he had had to answer the same question, he could have just done that. Ideally he would have used pen and paper, but an acceptable response would be to use the phone. The *least* acceptable response would have been to ask for a calculator. If you ask me for a calculator, then I am back in control, because I can say no. **It is not about what, it's about how. How do you deal with the issue?**

If you go back to the ashtray or the mobile phone exercise, you could throw it right back to me. 'What are you looking for that would convince you to make a decision today? What are the key features that are important to you?' The minute you ask those questions, I am going to start feeding you the lines, and I've done the job for you.

It reinforces one of my key beliefs: people generally think the strength lies in the answer, whereas I want to emphasize that **the skill is in finding the right question.**

> ### The JC twist
>
> When somebody is interviewing you for a job, there is a tendency to assume that just because they are on the other side of the desk they are an experienced interviewer – this is not always true. Their lack of experience may mean they ask a load of questions not related to the job on offer. Don't let them get away with it, because the interviewer will only remember that you didn't talk about the job – even if it's their fault you didn't. Steer the conversation back to the job, ask them about the key qualities and skills they are looking for, and then tell them why you have those in abundance.

When I was running a recruitment company, I would often sit in front of a client who was describing the person he was hoping to hire. He'd be telling me, 'This candidate has got to be the best, a high achiever,' describing an amazing person – because, of course, they all do. I'd look at him and say, 'The problem is, if I put the right candidate in front of you, you wouldn't be able to hire them. How are you going to attract that candidate to want to work for you? I'm not getting those vibes from you. Now, I do this for a living. I'm used to dealing with the kind of candidate you're describing, and if that candidate is already doing very well, if he's already working for one of your competitors, I am going to have to headhunt him to come and work for you. So why is he going to come to work for you?' If you want to hire a really good person, you have to be quite good yourself. Good people don't work for average people.

Going one step further

Let's say the first interview went well and you have been called back for a second appointment. You've now got the interview booked. What's stopping you from calling again and saying, 'I'm really looking forward to the next meeting. When we met, you mentioned that there were twelve people in the department. I am just wondering, James, would it be possible for me to meet somebody who I would be working with?' What could I say? It is difficult for me to say no.

Imagine you do meet somebody in the department. The chances of you then not getting the job are very slim. Because, all of a sudden, the information that is now available to you gives you the best possible chance of getting the job. You are going to meet someone you can ask, 'What do you do? Tell me about the department. Tell me what the last guy was like: what were his strengths, what were his weaknesses? How long have *you* been here? What are the key characteristics that you think people who succeed here have in common?'

Even if you have only twenty minutes with someone from the department, they could tell you everything you want to know. And when you walk into that second interview, you are in a strong position – if not a stronger position than the interviewer.

You have arrived with new information, you have moved on in your knowledge from the first interview. Fantastic. Of course the company could say it is not possible for you to meet anyone. But even if they did, I think they would admire you for asking the question. I would. It shows tremendous confidence to be able to ask that question.

If the interview process is proceeding well, you may then be invited to come along to a social event. 'Let's pop down to the pub,' the interviewer says. It happens a lot. And what do most people do? They drop their guard. They think they've got the job. It's understandable. But you haven't got the job, because you haven't got an offer letter.

If you do go out with the team, even though you are not sitting in an office, you are still being interviewed. It is simply an interview that is being held in a different location. Because the meeting is taking place in a social environment, people think it's easier, but it's not. The pitch to the candidate is always the same: 'Why don't you pop over on Thursday? We're going out for a bite with some of the guys from the office. Do join us – it will give you a chance to meet the team.' That's exactly how I would pitch it, very casually.

When you turn up on the evening, you will be sitting there with five people listening to everything you say, watching you very, very intently, though you might be oblivious to their level of interest. If I have asked some of my staff to go along, what do you think I will have said to them in advance? Am I going to say, 'Oh, we're going to have a bite to eat with John. It will be a good laugh. You should come along.' Or do you think I'm going to say,

'We've just interviewed this guy. I think he's quite interesting, so I've invited him along and I want to see what you think.'

The minute any boss says, 'I want to know what you think,' that is a very big clue – interview John. The next day, they know I'm going to ask them all what they think of John; it's pretty obvious.

Most people forget all the basics. Ninety per cent of people lose it at that point. And all because they have been taken out of the interview environment. They lose concentration, become too casual, too friendly, too familiar. They might drink more than they should, say more than they should, and not ask enough questions.

What you *should* be doing is the opposite. Still be friendly, be chatty, but remember why you are there. If the invitation had been worded differently – 'What I'd like you to do is come over on Thursday for a panel interview with the team that you're going to be working with' – your approach would be very different. But that's *exactly* what I mean. So you need to be very aware of how you should perform.

You have to interact with each of them. 'So, Brian, tell me what you do. What's your role in the company? Anne, how long have you been with the company, and what are your thoughts on where the company is headed?'

Just as in a formal job interview, you should aim to ask as many questions as they ask you. Even if they tell you nothing, but you've interviewed each of them, you have scored all the points. The feedback the staff are going to give their boss is, 'I thought the guy was very good.' They have to say that, because they didn't ask anything themselves. **You controlled the process.**

It is the same technique you would use for a panel interview. The key to panel interviews is to take control. It is hard – but if you don't, you will get squashed. Because generally you won't know who the people on the panel are.

As you come in and they start the process, you say, 'Would you mind if I ask a few questions?'

What do you think they're going to say? They'll say, 'Of course not.'

'So, John, what's your role in the company, and what are you looking for out of this interview today?'

Listen to his answer and he has just told you exactly what you need to do.

'What about you, Bill? How many other people are you going to be seeing today?'

You may find yourself in a situation where there are two people in the interview with you: the main interviewer and somebody from HR for the sake of compliance. If the HR person is genuinely there as an observer, they won't say very much. So it would be inappropriate to engage with them. But clearly if they do chip in on some of the points or raise some follow-up questions, and are more proactive, that suggests to me they might have an opinion about the interview too, and at the right moment you should draw them in, though being quite careful not to shift the emphasis away from your primary dialogue with the interviewer.

Going out on top

At the end of an interview, you can continue to retain control.
Ask another killer question: 'Would you mind if I asked you how
you feel the interview went?'

The beauty is, it can only go two ways. Either the interviewer
is going to say, 'It's been very useful, I think you've come across
very well,' which is reassuring for you. Or he'll say, 'We're very
impressed with you and we'd certainly want to call you back,
but we're still a bit concerned that your financial background is
not as strong as we were looking for.' Or, 'Actually I'm not sure
that your IT skills have come through at the interview.' Fantastic,
there's your cue. That's perfect, because by asking the question,
you've just found out why you were going to be rejected.

If you don't ask that particular question, you don't have
a chance to change the odds. This is all about adjusting the
balance of power. So, that question is critical in my mind.
Absolutely critical. 'How have I done?'

An even harder variation of that question – because you
have to be confident that you can take the feedback – is, 'Do
you have any reservations about my application?' Now, that is
a particularly tough thing to ask, but imagine if you did have
the confidence to ask the question, how powerful it would be
and how useful in helping you secure the job. If the interviewer
tells you what their principal reservation is, you have a chance
of turning the position. And if you didn't ask the question, you
wouldn't know.

This is all about psychology and timing. When I'm pitching for business and we've finished the pitch and wrapped it up, generally somebody from the meeting will walk out with me to reception or the lifts. I'll say, quite low-key, **What's your gut feeling?**

It's a brilliant question. I ask it every single time. And every single time it has the desired effect: they will tell you, simply because of the way the question is phrased. 'What's your gut feeling?' It is so open-ended.

Nine times out of ten they tell me something that proves vital. They give me a nugget. They might say, 'James, I thought it was really good, but I think you're going to be a bit expensive.' That tells me exactly how to follow up the pitch. But they would never tell me that negative in the meeting. People don't, because it is confrontational.

You can apply exactly the same technique when you are being shown out after an interview. 'How did I do? What's your gut feeling? Am I right for the company?' I know some people think that is too aggressive, too pushy. I buy all of that, other than the fact that, if you don't ask, you could have blown the interview, never know why and never have the chance to respond. *You'll never know.* That's the difference: I *want* to know. If I haven't got the job, I want to know why.

The ninety seconds you have as you are accompanied back to the reception area is a critical window in the whole process. Because you and the interviewer have left the meeting room, folded up your files, the normal guards are down. If you are really smart, you will not waste the opportunity.

An alternative tack is to say, as you're walking along, 'I just want to take this opportunity to say I've really enjoyed meeting you. I want to thank you because you made me feel really comfortable. And certainly, after the way you described the opportunity and the company, this is exactly what I'm looking for. I've got a really good feeling about the company: I think it's an environment somebody like me could really excel in.' In the interview itself, you probably didn't have the chance to explain whether you wanted the job or not, since most interviewers don't actually ask that directly. They've been too busy checking how many years you spent at each of your jobs. The interviewer is often sitting there, thinking, 'They're really good – I wonder if they'd accept the job if we offered it?' but not knowing for sure. You have just given them the confirmation they need. They'll come back with, 'Oh, thank you, I really appreciate that. It's good to know that if the job was offered to you, you'd accept.' And if there's still time, you can move on quite naturally to ask them what their feeling is.

Whatever you do, don't let your own guard drop: everything you do is still being clocked. Retain your professionalism until you are out of eyesight. Don't blow all your good work as you reach the exit, by looking at your watch and saying, 'Must dash, I've got another interview in half an hour, and I *really* don't want to miss that one ...'

Let me leave you with a question I was asked recently. I was interviewing somebody for Hamilton Bradshaw, and the candidate rounded off the interview by asking me, 'How does the interview process here work? How many interviews do you normally have – is it one, two or three?'

I said, 'Normally we go for three interviews.'

'And typically how many people would you see?'

'Six to eight.'

'How many have you seen for this particular position?'

'Five.'

Then he said, 'Can I ask one more question?'

'Sure.'

And this was a brilliant question. 'Is there anything you have seen in somebody else that you haven't seen in me?'

I had to smile, because it left me nowhere to go. Of course, I had to stop and reflect. Whatever I said was going to give my position away. I said, 'Just run that question by me again?' because I needed some time to think. The truth of the matter was that I had *not* seen anything in anybody else. I decided to be honest and tell him that.

His response was, 'In that case, is there any reason why I shouldn't be invited back for a second interview?'

I had to say, 'No.'

'Great,' he said. 'Shall I see your PA on the way out and confirm a time that's good for you?'

Again, I had to give him the answer he was looking for. 'Fine.'

He closed me perfectly. And of course, when I was going through the CVs, that incident stood out in my mind, above anything else that had happened in the interviews with the other candidates.

And he'd got what he wanted: that second interview. More power to his elbow.

'The single biggest reason most people accept job offers is because they like the person who interviewed them — and this works both ways.'

152   GET THE JOB YOU REALLY WANT

8. PLEASURE

A job interview, fun? Most people would scoff at the very thought. But that's because we are preprogrammed to think of them as gruelling experiences. TV reality shows have done their bit to give the impression that every job application should be a fight to the death and a confidence-sapping experience. But that's not reality, that's entertainment.

I want to encourage you to turn your preconceptions of the job interview on their head. My inspirational mentor, Tom O'Dwyer, who I worked for at the Reid Trevena recruitment agency, had a real knack for showing candidates a dream, and inspiring them. If you can get the interviewer to inspire *you* with their plans for the company and the job they are offering, both of you will have a sense of enjoyment that can prove infectious.

I have talked about the vital importance of preparation so that you feel completely relaxed, informed and confident, of thinking through all aspects of how you present yourself so that you make a strong, friendly first impression, and of not letting the interviewer's power games or curve-ball questions get to you.

But even with all that ammunition, you may suddenly feel wobbly or uncertain at some point in the interview, and that can trigger an outburst of nerves. Part of it may be down to tiredness. Perhaps you've been doing several interviews over the past few days and the strain is kicking in. But you may be the twenty-fourth candidate this interviewer has seen, and they will be feeling jaded too. Why not be the one who brings some energy back into the interview?

Come into the room with a realistic approach: don't bank everything on this particular position. Because if you give it your best shot and you don't get the job, then maybe, just maybe, the job was not the right one for you.

One sure-fire way to keep a positive and upbeat mood is to avoid moaning about your current job, or complaining in general. If the first thing you do at an interview is to blame the dreadful state of public transport for your late arrival, and then carry on bleating about your current boss because he doesn't understand quite how talented you are, and round it off by explaining that one of the reasons you want to leave your job is that one of the other staff members is holding a grudge against you, the interviewer is more than likely going to conclude that the problem is not with everybody else – it's with you.

Whatever else happens during the interview, you want to go out on an upbeat note, and leave behind the impression that you always wanted the job, but that you now want it even more after meeting and talking to the interviewer. Be pleasant, but not overfriendly – you're not trying to be best mates after one meeting.

Overcoming nerves

To make the interview process pleasurable for both sides, the secret lies in creating a sense of relaxation, and establishing that rather mystical, indefinable quality: *rapport*. This should arise naturally from the knowledge you have acquired in advance, and the confidence that knowledge automatically gives you. But the pressure of the interview situation can still lead to nerves, which will obscure all the good work you have put in.

Since appearing on *Dragons' Den*, I have noticed – and I find this quite astonishing – that ninety per cent of the people who come and see me now are incredibly nervous and uncomfortable, simply because they perceive me as a TV celebrity. They have seen me on TV, read about me in the newspapers. These are people who are successful in their own right – and yet, when they walk into my office, to some degree they are shaking.

And because I am an experienced interviewer, I can spot those nerves a mile away.

In that situation I will ask the interviewee, 'Are you feeling nervous?'

At this point most people will say, 'Actually, you know, I am a bit nervous.'

It is a relief for them to admit that.

'Listen,' I'll say. 'Relax. Would you like something to drink?'

I'll completely change the subject and always add a gentle touch of humour. I will stop whatever is going on. If you're there to sell to me, I'll do something different. If you're trying to interview me, we'll take a break from the formal conversation.

I need to take you out of this zone because, if I'm interviewing you, I can't really work you out. Your nerves are disguising who you are. I am struggling to evaluate you. I need to know about you, but your nerves are creating a shield. I am in danger of picking up the wrong message. **Do I think any the less of you because you are nervous? No, I don't.**

I think this is a very important message. Because your display of nerves tells me that you care. Generally when people are nervous in a job interview, it's because they really want the job. Obviously all candidates set out with the aim of hiding their nerves. They don't want me to notice. But if I do, it's not a bad thing, because my reading of it is that you clearly want the job.

So, don't crumble. Don't feel you've failed. It's part of human behaviour. Don't be disconcerted by it. If it happens, just deal with it. If you feel flustered, and you have the strength of mind, you can always say, 'Oh, could you give me a minute, could I have some water?' You need to buy yourself a little time.

I once turned up for an interview and felt very intimidated, because I had imagined I was going for an interview with one person, and when I walked in I saw it was a panel of four.

There were four chairs with another one in front for me. It felt completely wrong.

I sat down, felt totally fazed, and immediately said, 'Excuse me, can I use the bathroom for a second?'

'Of course.'

I needed to get out of there, because I knew that if I carried on I was going to blow the interview anyway. The panel would see that I was very uncomfortable.

I left the room, went to the bathroom, splashed some cold water on my face, composed myself mentally, regrouped in my head. I went straight back in again, and this time I was a totally different person, because now I knew what I was walking into. I had reprogrammed my mind, repositioned myself for the event I was entering. I was better prepared.

I have talked about trying to introduce a note of humour to ease the pressure of the interview. If you feel that you have the ability, the style and the personality, you should be able to find a moment where you can introduce an element of humour. That will only work in your favour, not against you, as long as you don't turn out to be a comedian and devalue what you are doing. You can achieve the same effect by bringing a feel-good factor to the interview.

Somebody came in to pitch to me the other day. He sat down, and said, 'By the way, James, I've brought you a coffee,' and placed a Starbucks cup on the table – a fantastic ice-breaker.

I was quite taken aback and asked him, 'How did you know what kind of coffee I prefer?'

He said, 'Well, I got you a latte, to be on the safe side.'

'OK,' I said. 'But did you get it with sugar or without?'

Very cleverly he came back with, 'Which would you like?' He'd brought some sugar and a stirrer along with him.

All the way through the meeting, that incident stuck in my head. Clearly he had thought about doing something a little out of the ordinary. You usually walk into a meeting and are asked if you'd like to have tea, coffee or water. But by bringing the drinks in himself, he had turned the idea on its head.

It will add to your score if you can do something different like that. The minute you can find the one thing that brings the meeting – and you – to life, that is when you can show a glimpse of your passion. Sometimes it can be very hard to be passionate about yourself, so you need to discover the items, the triggers that will raise your tempo.

Depending on the nature of the job, you could bring along to the interview something visual that you have created, or articles about your achievements. If you've made something, produced something tangible, that always goes down well in a meeting. I usually find that an interview held across acres of empty desk can be rather stark.

You could bring in a prop to do with the company you are visiting. If it's a fashion company, maybe there's a particular garment that they have made. Or if the company produces books or games, you could have an example of the product range with you. The very fact that you have brought something in with you will set the interview apart in the interviewer's mind.

I always use a lot of props throughout any interview process. If you come for an interview with me, it will never be simply 'An Interview'. I will bring other people into the meeting. I will get you to pop downstairs to meet somebody else in the office. I'll give you a guided tour of the building. I'll show you some documents which explain what the company has done and how it reached its current position.

I work hard to make the interview very interactive, very warm, because I am trying to engage you. My objective as someone who is in a hiring position is that whenever I interview somebody who turns out to be very good, I want to be 100 per cent sure that if I then offer them the job, they will take it. Whether I want to hire you or not is a different issue – when I am talking to employers, my message is always that they should only hire the best of every batch they see.

The employer has to sell themselves to the candidate too. Imagine you go for an interview with two different companies as an account executive, and both jobs sound attractive and the salaries are equal. But one of the interviewers is charming, friendly, engaging and genuinely interested in your skills and your personality, and the other interviewer is very formal and process-driven. If they both offered you the job, which one would you accept?

How often does the interviewer get the best candidate? Not that often. I know that for a fact, because as a recruitment consultant I was often the person pre-screening and then sending the candidates over for an interview with the client, and I would be astonished just how often the hirer failed to secure the pick of each particular bunch. During my debrief with the client, the employer would always believe it was the occasion, or something about the package on offer. Not true: nine times out of ten it was because the employer had not connected with the candidate, had simply not engaged.

If you are the interviewee, my message to you is the same. You need to engage, because you want to succeed at every interview you go to.

Of course you are there to be interviewed for the job, but remember what is going through the mind of the person interviewing you. It's not just about whether you can do the job, but one of the most important questions in the interviewer's mind is, **Will you fit in?**

What are you bringing to *their* party?

How many times do candidates fail to get selected and then say they can't understand it? In their own mind they believe they are perfect for the job. You can be perfect on paper, but you won't be offered the job if you haven't presented yourself as someone who is able to integrate naturally within a team environment – whether that's because of personality, or style, or lack of communication skills. If you are not able to relax, use an element of humour – if you're not able to put yourself across in terms other than purely recounting your work experience, I think that even with the perfect CV you will struggle.

I have seen it myself. I've been interviewing a candidate and have gone through their CV. They tick all the boxes, but for some reason I am not clicking with them, not warming to them. Maybe it's because they are too stiff.

The interview is not about what is happening on one particular day. You could be working for me for five years. You could be here for ten years. This is actually quite a big decision for me as the employer. I have to work out whether you will fit into our environment. How does the interviewer evaluate that?

And how do you, the interviewee, communicate that? By being yourself, by being somebody who is warm, by being friendly, by opening up, by giving the impression that you are approachable. If I come away with the impression that you are too stiff, that you are not somebody who is going to gel in my team, that worries me. I have to create a happy environment. There is a culture in this organization. Do you fit into that?

Identifying with the company culture

The culture of an organization is one aspect of a company that is very difficult to glean from even the most comprehensive website. It doesn't translate easily into words and images. It hovers just beneath the surface.

I believe that organizations, especially under pressure in a difficult economic climate, often forget that the workplace is not just about somebody coming into work, doing their job, making a contribution, getting paid. That is not the reason staff stay with a company. I find that company bosses talk a great deal about 'culture' but don't have any convincing answers when I ask them what they are actively doing as an employer to develop and manage that culture.

If you approach a staff member in a successful organization, and offer them more money and a better position, one of the key reasons they *won't* leave is because they have made strong friendships inside their existing company. That is really hard to break. If you like the people you work with, the environment you're in, if the company has a great culture, and it feels like a family, I won't be able to move you for love or money. I've been doing this for twenty-five years. I know you won't leave. The money on offer might be significantly more, the career opportunities more exciting, but you feel as though you're letting people down.

I have had a situation where I've sent somebody for an interview and they've been offered the job. I've called the person back in and said, 'Talk me through your resignation process . . .' and straight away I can see it in their face.

'Actually, you know, James, I'm not entirely sure.'

When they think about the resignation process, about handing their notice in, they're not thinking about the HR person, they're thinking, 'What's Phil going to say? What's Julie going to think?' They are part of a team, they contribute to a team, so suddenly it's about letting those people down. And there's a good likelihood – because the chances are they would be leaving to join a competitor – that they feel like a traitor.

Joining the culture club

Now company culture doesn't just happen, it has to be created. The organization needs to understand what sort of culture they are trying to create. What *is* the personality of the organization? And once that culture has been created, what are they doing to maintain it?

Is the company a good place to come and work in? Often it is the smallest, the most basic things that contribute to that. Is there a kitchen in the office? Is there a toaster? Some people like coming in early. When they do, can they make their own breakfast? All this is part of the culture of the company.

If you look at Google, their whole environment is about the Google culture. When you turn up for an interview at Google, they're not even selling the brand, they're selling the culture. It's all very relaxed, everybody's dressed casually, there's a pool table in the corner ... To my mind, that culture didn't just happen. Nobody got up in the morning and found it had arrived by its own volition. The company clearly thought about the kind of people they wanted. They said, 'People perform well when they are happy. People perform well when they are chilled. People perform better because they've got friends and they like who they work with.' The whole culture of Google is based around that.

I have come across many companies where the directors think that creating company culture is all to do with holding an annual conference, or the Christmas do. They plan a big event, spend a lot of money, but it feels rather staged. I am much keener on regular small-scale events. They are far more effective. It could be having a massage bench in one of the rooms and asking somebody to come in once a month to offer fifteen-minute shoulder massages – nothing too grand, but it has an impact, because it's different, it's fun.

In one of my organizations we will take a whole team go-karting. Now, it's not actually about the go-karting per se, but about spending time together outside the working environment, creating real friendships, strengthening the bonds between people, letting them gel naturally. And say that Sally-Ann from the production department gets the fastest time, everybody now sees her in a completely different light. Or we'll go off to a comedy club – £15 a head – just a bunch of us sitting there for two and a half hours, laughing our heads off.

When somebody comes along for an interview, if they talk to an employee in the company and ask them what it's like working there, the employee won't talk about the job function, they'll say, 'Oh, it's great, last month we all went go-karting, and you'll never believe it, Sally-Ann from Production beat all the boy racers hands down!' Or, 'On Friday we went to the Comedy Club and we had such a laugh. We all came back and went to a club afterwards.' I've seen it happen time and time again. When people interact and enjoy themselves, they want to talk about it, because it stands out.

So, from your point of view, what can you do to establish whether the culture of the company you want to join is a culture you can relate to, a culture you can feel comfortable being part of? Maybe you can arrange one of your interviews early in the morning as people arrive – a good way to gauge the atmosphere.

But most easily, as part of your questioning of the interviewer, you can ask these questions:

- 'How would you describe the culture of your organization, James?'
- 'What makes you different as an organization from the others?'
- 'How often do the staff get together outside work?'
- 'Is there much of a social environment here, or is it pretty much all about work?'

The answer is really simple. As always – and I *will* keep banging away on this point – **ask the question!**

The JC twist

I read the other day that fewer than thirty per cent of interviewees ever write to the person who has interviewed them to say thank you. In an age of instant emails why not jot a short, polite, personal and handwritten note and post it within twenty-four hours? Even if it doesn't tip the balance, you'll be remembered as somebody with gracious manners, and should that job or a similar one come up again, you will have left a positive memory.

"If a job interview doesn't go your way, don't dwell on it. Immediately look for what you can learn from the experience. Come away stronger."

9. PERSEVERANCE

As an investor, I have had to learn that not every deal succeeds. The same is true of interviews. I would love to guarantee you 100 per cent success – and I think we can get close – but not every interview will end with you getting the job. So, how do you pick up the pieces and lift yourself back up if you *do* miss out on a job?

I was recently contacted by a British-born man who had returned to the UK after a number of years working in Australia. He was motivated, he had been successful and had plenty of experience, but he could not find work in the UK.

He told me that all the companies he was contacting were frightened away by his foreign experience, and that apparently they could not see how it was relevant to their UK needs. He felt he was stuck, had run out of ideas on where to go next, and asked for my advice.

'You're forgetting an important lesson,' I told him. 'Always trade on your skills. Think of the interview as a business transaction. The interviewer has a job to sell, and you have the skills with which to pay. The employer wants to get the most he or she possibly can for the job – who wouldn't? – so you have to maximize the value of your skills, in other words "pay" more.'

I suggested he apply to Australian companies operating in the UK, to make the most of that overseas experience. In that context he was suddenly increasing the value of his experience. It was a question of taking stock, and persevering.

First of all, though, I want to remind you that sometimes having the right combination of determination and focus *is* enough.

When my daughter Hanah was applying to go to university, she came to me and said, 'Dad, I've filled in the admissions form.'

I took a look at the six options she had put down. As option number 1 she had written down 'London School of Economics', for option number 2 'LSE' again – 3, 4, 5 and 6, all 'LSE'.

I should have known better, but I underestimated her. I said, 'Darling, it doesn't work like that. The reason why there are six options is because the chances are you may not get your first choice, which is why you need to spread your bets.'

'But,' she said, 'I only want to go to LSE.'

I said, 'What happens if you don't get in?'

'Well, I'll take a gap year and try again.'

She was 100 per cent committed. She did her research, she met students who were already studying there, she understood what the LSE's expectations were. Because that was the only place where she wanted to study, she didn't leave a stone unturned.

Where did she end up going? LSE.

So yes, if you do the job right, the chances are it will work. If you come 100 per cent prepared to *Dragons' Den*, if you understand the process, if you research your market and your competition, if you know your numbers, if you've done all the things you should do, you have changed the odds in favour of you getting an investment.

But . . . if you *don't* get the job you thought you wanted, then make sure you ask for feedback. During the early stages of setting up Alexander Mann I went out of my way to get feedback. If I received negative feedback, I took stock and changed the agency's selling point. And if the customer was happy, I could use their positive feedback to my advantage. In the job process, if you fail to get selected, assess why you weren't chosen and be prepared to deal with any issues you can identify.

Let's say you receive a letter that says, 'Thank you for coming in, but unfortunately you haven't been selected.' The first thing you should be thinking about is finding out why. Nine out of ten companies will not give you a reason in the letter, and most people accept that. But remember that I am significantly more self-critical than most, and therefore I am *not* going to accept it. I want to know why. Because **if I don't know why, how am I going to improve?**

For some people, getting a job is a process: 'I've been for three interviews. I might not get the job, but it doesn't matter.

I'll go for another one.' That is not my mindset. If I didn't get the job, I want to know why I didn't get it.

Leave it a day or two and call back. But if I call the HR person, they'll never tell me; they'll give me some standard response. I want to talk to the person who interviewed me. If I call to ask why I didn't get the job, they're going to feel uncomfortable, because human nature is such that people don't want to engage in a negative discussion. The situation needs some finesse.

So, I would ring and say, 'Hi, we met the other day about the job in sales. I understand you've offered the position to somebody else. I fully understand the situation. You must have seen a lot of people. But, just out of curiosity, could I ask you: what was the one thing that made me unsuitable for the role? What was it that didn't quite do the trick?'

Most people don't have the confidence to engage in that conversation.

The other person will try and fob you off with a bland answer: 'You didn't have the right experience.'

That's the time to push harder: 'Was there any particular area where you think my experience was limited?' I'm not going to give up, I'm going to wear them down. 'Specifically, where did I not have the experience – was it in sales, or marketing, or on the financial side?'

'Well, we felt that although you were good at sales, we were looking for somebody to work on the corporate accounts, and we just didn't feel you had that level of experience.'

Bingo. Now I have something to work with. They hadn't told me that in the interview. And it just so happens that, for my previous employer, I won Vodafone as a client, which is one of the largest accounts we have. In the interview we were mainly talking about performance, not necessarily about the size of key customers. But that's useful to know. That tells me that although the mistake was the interviewer's for not asking, whatever else happens I have learned a valuable lesson. For any future interviews, rather than only talking about my perform- ance in sales, I ought to go into more detail about the type of customers I have won. Obviously it was very important to the interviewer, but he didn't draw it out of me.

> ### The JC twist
>
> If, when I called to find why I hadn't got a job, they gave me a particular reason, what I wouldn't do at that point is pitch back against that point. Because that's what everybody's going to do. You can't help it: you want to correct that impression straight away. Don't do it. Because you should never do what they expect you to do. Their guard is up. The minute they give you a reason, they know you're going to come straight back at them. And the fact that they know you're going to do that means they have switched off. Plus, whatever you say will only score 5 out of 10, because you haven't thought about it. When you respond that quickly, your argument won't be great.

When the interviewer has finished giving me their feedback, I would say, 'Thank you very much, that's very useful. I really appreciate your time,' and put the phone down.

Now they're surprised. I've really thrown them. They are confused because I have done something they absolutely did not expect me to do.

I would then write back. That gives me time to consider, to reflect on what they have said, and time to compose the response. The key thing here is not to criticize their decision. I would word the letter, or email, along the following lines.

Thank you for taking the time to speak to me yesterday. I really appreciate your honesty. I have had a chance to reflect on the things you said, and I can clearly see how you came to make your decision. It is probably my fault, because I didn't explain myself clearly enough. But when I was at this particular company, one of the key focuses of my job covered exactly the area of your concern about my experience. As a result of that focus, these are the things I achieved there that made a significant difference to the company's success . . .

Because you now know the element you were missing in the interview, you have the chance to demonstrate very specifically that you do have the experience they thought was missing. Now, I'm not saying they are going to call you tomorrow and offer you the job, but the odds have certainly improved in your favour.

You can always tilt the balance towards you by establishing what the window of opportunity would be if you don't make the cut – in other words, how much time have you got before they make their final decision and the opportunity has disappeared? Ask, 'Could you talk me through your recruitment process? Is it typically a two-interview or a three-interview process? How long would that process take? And when would you like the ideal candidate to start?'

Responding to redundancy

If you have recently been made redundant, the question of perseverance and resilience is doubly important. I have interviewed many, many people who have been made redundant, and I find, more often than not, that one of the reasons they are finding it tough to get another job is that the job function they used to carry out is now much harder to find. I always recommend that before anybody dives into the job market they analyse how the job function they previously filled is performing within that particular industry in general. If you were working in the music business as the sales manager responsible for CD sales, there won't be many vacancies for CD sales executives any more. That part of the industry is dying. The job function is disappearing.

Take a calm, considered look at your former job. Did it disappear because the company was performing badly, because the industry was going through a tough period, or because the job function is now outdated? The world evolves, and we have to adapt. Take retailing. Not that long ago, if you were a retailer with a hundred stores, you would automatically plan to grow the business to 150 stores. It was the natural order of things in that sector. So, there were always new opportunities for staff as new stores opened. Now the business is contracting. Store managers who used to move regularly are not leaving as often as they used to, because finding another similar job is not easy. And one of the key reasons for this is the rise and rise of online retailing.

Even I have been shocked by the sale of an online company like Net-A-Porter, valued at around £350 million. If you had asked me ten years ago, 'James, do you think women will be buying clothes online?' my answer would have been, 'Absolutely not.' Because I had grown up in a world where traditional sense said that we need to feel clothes, we want to try them on, before buying them. But in fact the answer, as we now know, is 'Yes, people will happily buy clothes online.' With those kinds of changes under way you have to re-evaluate your own job function, and assess the extent to which your skills are comparable to and compatible with other market areas.

The element of persistence that you need after a redundancy is not about simply soldiering on, not a stiff-upper-lip approach of sending out 400 CVs and taking 400 rejection letters on the chin, but of being persistent in thinking laterally and exploring the other industries where your skill set and your experience are relevant.

Turning a job down

If you are not happy with any aspect of the job, turn it down. This could play into your hands. You may find that it is the hirer who perseveres, because they have seen something in you which matches exactly what they are looking for, and they are prepared to address whatever it is that has been holding you back from accepting the job.

I was headhunting somebody as chief executive for a company, and offered him the position. He turned it down.

I really, really wanted this guy, so I left it for a week, rang him up and said, 'Hi, Gavin. I understand you've turned the position down. I totally understand the situation, and I am quite happy to accept it. I suppose we've both moved on now, because you're going to stay where you are, and I'm interviewing other people . . .' I paused and then asked, 'What was the key reason you turned it down?'

He said it was all to do with share options.

I never saw that one coming. I asked him to expand on that.

He said, 'Well, I've got some options in the company where I am at the moment. I felt I couldn't walk away from those.'

'OK.' I asked, 'What are the options worth?'

'If we do x over the next three years,' he answered, 'they'll be worth y.'

I said, 'Fine. Do you have any certainty or guarantee that in the next three years you will deliver x for the options to be worth the figure you've just given me?'

He admitted he did not.

I said, 'If you took the job we have on offer, the forecast for the business you gave us during the interview process was this. Based on those figures your stake is worth three times your current options. And your current options are based on the entire company [he was working for a public company] performing, something which you're not in control of. With the equity I could offer you, you *would* be in control, because you'd be the chief executive. If I was in your position, I'd want something that I could influence and I could control.

'Now the sixty-four million dollar question for you, Gavin, is this: how deliverable do you think your forecast is? Because if you don't believe in that, I would stay where you are. I would totally agree with your decision. But if you do believe your forecast is deliverable, then this is a no-brainer.'

He said, 'I hadn't looked at it that way. I think you make a really good point. Would you mind if we had a coffee? Because I would like to talk through that in some more detail.'

I got him back in again, we went through the numbers, he accepted the position, joined and did amazingly well.

The key point was that I didn't give up. I went back to ask the question.

Learning from your mistakes

In life generally, I find that people take successes in their stride, but they tend to learn more from their mistakes. If something you are working on goes well, you don't analyse it, you just move on to the next project or deal. But if it doesn't work, you stop and ask the question. You want to understand it, analyse it. I always learn far more from the deals that go wrong than from the deals that go right. My development and my improvement arise from my failures, not from my successes.

The number of mistakes you make is in line with how successful you become. Without a question. More success comes with better technique. You don't become more successful by going backwards. **How do you become better, if you don't learn from the mistakes you make?**

If I hadn't addressed my demons and my phobias, I would never have broken the mould. I would never have learned a thing. There is not one day that goes by when I don't realize that I've screwed up, said the wrong thing, done the wrong thing. But I address my mistakes, I learn from my mistakes. The key factor for me is that I don't make those same mistakes again. I make different mistakes.

By being driven, by being hungry, I want to be better. I am prepared to do something about it. For most people, those are just words. To me, they mean something. And in that quest to be better, how do you become better if you don't question? You have to question – not just others, but yourself.

I think that everybody, in every job function within an organization, can do that. If an employer ever lets you go, irrespective of what reason you are given, I would argue that more often than not it is because you don't perform, you don't contribute and you are not delivering.

You might hear about cutbacks, or that the company is scaling down. But I have sat through dozens, maybe hundreds of meetings advising the board of an organization which is downsizing. It is the same in every situation – you go through a list of people and very quickly it becomes clear who is dispensable and who is *in*dispensable. I would love it if the employees could sit in on those meetings, because they would soon realize that the conversations are not rocket science.

The board goes through the list and someone asks, 'So, how's Bob doing?'

'Oh, we can't let Bob go. Bob does this, he does that, he brought us this customer, and he's grown that account ten times over.'

It takes five minutes, and everybody agrees that Bob has got to stay.

You move on to another name on the list, and this time the feedback is, 'Well, he's not doing very much for us at the moment. He's not really contributing.'

The decision is so easy, but it is because that person made it easy. He gifted them the opportunity to let him go.

A great tester is when somebody goes off on a two-week holiday, and nothing changes. There's a big message there. In one of our businesses somebody took a three-week holiday and then their return was delayed, so they weren't actually working in the business for a month.

While they were away, I was talking to their manager, asking, 'How's that function going?' I expected him to say, 'We've got a few issues, and I've had to bring in some cover to make sure everything stays on track while so and so's away.'

Instead, he answered, 'Actually, it's fine.'

I said, 'What do you mean, "It's fine"?'

By telling me everything was fine, what I was hearing was that we were employing somebody who could be away from that job for a month without it making any difference.

That evening the line manager's comment really bugged me, so the next morning I went in and asked him, 'Can you do me a favour? I want to review exactly what the output of that job is.'

When we looked at his review, we all came to the conclusion that there wasn't a job there. Technology had evolved to such an extent that the job had become a process role, and the manager had demonstrated that there was enough bandwidth in the department, that we didn't really need that person any more. Funnily enough, that job no longer exists . . .

So, you can apply an attitude of persistence and perseverance not only to getting a new job but also to the job you are in right now. You have to understand that there is no organization that I've ever come across that doesn't have its own politics. If you have an achievement, you should make it known so that when the next promotion comes up, there are people other than your manager who think you are talented.

Understand the components of the next level up from your current position, and start to demonstrate that you can do some of those tasks. Ask to be given some of those responsibilities without the title. If you are an accounts assistant, and being an accounts manager means you have to do the monthly management accounts, ask your boss, 'Is it OK if I help put together the monthly accounts?' Or if you are a PA, volunteer to take the minutes at the next board meeting. If you can show that level of initiative and carry out some of the specific activities that happen at the next level up, your willingness to be involved will be noticed.

Although persevering if you believe a job should be yours is a valuable skill, you should also be prepared to admit when a job is not working out. I had a lawyer approach me a couple of years ago. He wanted to change careers, to come over and work in private equity. He was a senior partner, with a six-figure income to match. We thought it was too much of a risk. But he insisted: 'How would you feel if I took a sabbatical and came and tried the job?' We agreed and we gave him an opportunity. He tried the job for three months and it was pretty obvious at the end of that period that he wasn't suited to our industry.

A lawyer is trained to think in a very specific way, and sometimes you can't change that habit, you can't change the way you think. Lawyers have the ability to think in a way that is very critical and very analytical, which I don't think necessarily works in the private equity industry. At the end of the sabbatical, I told him I thought he should go back to law: 'I think that is really you; it's who you are.'

He was deeply disappointed, but in his heart of hearts he agreed. He had made such a big commitment, taking the sabbatical – quite a bold move for him. I am sure he would have loved things to work out. **But sometimes it's just as useful to know what you can't do as what you can.**

'Fantastic, it worked. You've been offered the job you really wanted. Congratulations. But before you celebrate too much, negotiate a deal that works for you.'

10. POKER

Whenever you get offered a job, there is always room for negotiation. It is easy to be carried away on the adrenalin rush of acceptance and forget to step back and take a cool, collected view of what the offer actually represents.

With the job offer in hand, it is time for you to evaluate the factors involved in deciding whether you want to accept it: the salary package and the related benefits are an obvious consideration. You could change those in the course of negotiating a final deal.

But there are some things you *can't* change. The company culture that I have talked about, for example – that is something you cannot alter. Did you feel comfortable when you went into the office? Could you identify with the company's aims? You can't change where the company is based. Will the commute be too long, too draining – if so, will you have to move house, and what impact will that have on your family, your kids? Your first decision is whether the job, the role, is right for you.

Once you have made your mind up, aim to negotiate a fair deal. Don't dither too much, or try to bluff too hard by claiming other fictitious job offers. And although you need a reasonable time to assess the offer, don't let it drag out.

If you are going to work for a company and perform well there, you want your new employers to feel positive towards you from day one, not resentful or slightly cheated. Secure a win-win package, then close the deal.

First of all, remember that a job offer is only that: an offer. It is not a deal until you have accepted it.

The only time the job is truly yours is the day you begin work. Even when you've had the final interview and the company is about to make you the offer, you haven't got the job. Even when they've made you that offer, the letter will always say somewhere that it is conditional upon a medical or upon references. Having run many recruitment companies, I can assure you that I have seen plenty of offers collapse in the period after the offer letter is sent out.

Supplying the right references

I have seen deals go down when the references were checked. In the job process each component plays an important part – and the referees you have supplied are equally critical. Unless you have spoken to the people you have given as referees, unless you have had the courtesy to contact them in advance and let them know they might expect a call, you may get a nasty surprise just when you least expect it.

Avoid the surprises. Bring your referees up to speed. Tell them about the company you're applying to, the job you have applied for, and how far you have got in the process.

'I've had two interviews so far. I'm not there yet, but I think they might call you. What are your thoughts about the position? Because, frankly, I'd like to know.'

If they're not confident that you are making the right move, it is far better for you to know early on.

The usual pattern of the conversation when an employer rings for a reference is, 'Oh, hi, I just want to know, did Bill work for you?'

'Yes, he did.'

'Was he with you for three years?'

'He was.'

'Was he any good at his job?'

'He was fine.'

'Would you rehire him?'

'Yes, we probably would.'

A series of bland, box-ticking questions.

When I call for a reference, I approach things differently. My phone call will go along these lines.

'Thanks for taking the time to speak to me. Bill is applying for a position here as a sales director. Now, in our organization a sales director's role is a, b, c and d. I wanted to ask you, from your experience having worked with Bill, is that a challenge you think he would rise to?' Or, 'In this particular position, Bill's going to be responsible for seventeen people. What was the size of team he managed with you?'

'Eight.'

'OK, so if in your organization you had to double the size of that team, how do you think Bill would have coped with that?'

I am very specific with my questions. And you would be surprised how many times the answer I get is, 'I'm not sure,' or, 'I don't think he could.' Which is exactly what I need to know. I am looking for real feedback on the candidate for the job that I am looking to fill.

I remember taking a reference on somebody I was hiring, and the referee was telling me, 'Yes, he was very good, he did this, he did that, he was here for three years.' I was getting nothing fresh, nothing useful to me.

Then I asked, 'Would you rehire him?'

There was a deathly silence at the other end of the line. Eventually, the referee said, 'Probably not.'

I thought, 'Aha!' and followed up with, 'Can I ask why?'

'Not really. I don't want to go into the details.'

I said, 'OK, I appreciate that. Would it be because of his ability in the job?'

'No, his ability was OK.'

'Was it the quality of his work?'

'No, not particularly.'

'So, was it his style?'

He said, 'You're getting warmer . . .'

My interpretation of that conversation was that the

candidate was not much of a team player. It just so happened that the job I had on offer focused on working in a close team of five people. So the referee's response left a doubt lingering in my mind. He had not really given a bad reference, but he had said enough, and what he *hadn't* said spoke volumes.

In that particular instance, we had already held the third interview, and I had told the candidate we were going to make him an offer, subject to references ... I had to have a swift rethink. I got him back in, and said, 'One of the things I want to share with you is that we do work in a very small team environment. It's very much a collective environment. Could you talk me through the dynamics of your previous job? How did you work and how did you get on with your team?' I spent a whole hour on that single subject.

And it became apparent that he was a bit of a loner, operating very much as an island, that he had not really been dependent on other people, and almost felt that other people were something of a distraction. That gave me enough of a specific reason to say that we had decided not to go ahead with the offer, which was a direct result of the reference that had pointed me in a particular direction.

It can be illegal to give a false or inaccurate reference. To avoid exposing themselves to any risk, most referees avoid stating outright that one of their employees was useless or incompetent. What they can do is say in answer to any question, 'No comment', or leave a large question mark hanging in the air.

The issue here is about value. I understand that a hiring

decision is a big decision. There is an operational risk, a commercial risk, an economic risk. And when people leave a company, staff become disaffected. It creates a bad environment. So, the consequences of getting any hiring decision wrong are significant.

Therefore, as an employer, I want to do everything I can to avoid making that mistake. I can't afford not to take up detailed references. Some employers don't put the same value on that as I do, and so they take a greater risk than I do. All I am trying to do is manage my risk better. Someone who has worked with the candidate for three years is a far better judge of character than I can be at that point. They know the person. I want to benefit from their knowledge.

And by the way, if your instincts tell you that something is wrong with the company who wants to hire you, act on it. If something is not right, don't be afraid to turn the offer down. A woman wrote to me telling me that she had been in an interview with a company director who would have been her boss had she taken the job. Halfway through the interview the director took a call from another staff member, and promptly started yelling back down the phone, ripping a strip off them. The interview continued, the job was offered to her – and she promptly turned it down. There was no way she could report to somebody who had that kind of attitude towards his staff. Thankfully that is a rare occurrence.

The traditional area of negotiation for a job offer has been salary level. The applicant assumes the employer has built in some margin for improvement, and that they will show their business acumen by holding out for more. After the recession, all the old rules and ways of doing things are up for grabs. Think laterally and surprise your new employer by asking for an improvement in the offer that doesn't cost them any more money but will give both you and them more value.

Negotiating the best deal for yourself

When you receive the offer, if financially it's not quite what you thought, should you accept that? The answer is: not necessarily.

You might start by saying, 'That's about where I am at the moment, but I'm getting ready to move house shortly and financially it would help me to have a higher level. Is there anything about my performance that you're particularly concerned about?'

Perhaps they might say, 'We don't think you have enough experience at this level.'

'Well, if I came to work with you for three months, and really proved to you beyond any reasonable doubt that I was exceptional, would you be prepared to give me a review after three months and, if you were convinced, to increase the salary to £50,000 at that point? Could you defer it and make it conditional?'

With that kind of pitch, the chances are you would get it. This is the time to secure that option. Because once you are embedded as part of the company, it is hard to get a salary increase. You have given away your bargaining position. While you're still sitting outside, your bargaining position is much stronger. The company have already said they want you, so you have succeeded in that part of the process. Now it's about agreeing a number.

Most employers have some flexibility on salary. And I always have that in the back of my mind. What is the range, the bandwidth of their leeway? If the job opportunity has come via an agency, you know there is a fee attached – between twenty per cent and twenty-five per cent of your first year's salary – and that reduces your bargaining power. But if you are in a situation where there is no fee, that gives you at least a twenty per cent margin to play with: I would spend a fair amount of time returning on that.

Managing expectations

If you pitch really hard on salary, that will subsequently increase the expectations of your employer. Because you can't negotiate a better deal without promising more, or confirming more. You don't negotiate by saying, 'Thanks for the £50,000 offer, but I really want £60,000.' You're not going to get it – somehow you'll have to explain or justify why you want more.

People promise the earth, 'I am going to perform better. I'm going to do this in the organization.' They over-promote their capability.

The employer says, 'Well, if you're really that much better, I'll give you £60,000.'

And then you join. You come in thinking, 'I've got the job now, I'm going to do my normal thing.'

The problem is, it's not a normal situation. Because you've forced the package twenty per cent higher than the norm. And because you've negotiated so high, everybody is expecting Wonder Boy or Wonder Woman to come in. And frankly, if you are not, you've done yourself an injustice, because you are going to fall flat on your face by not demonstrating the premium value you promised.

Throughout the interview process, it is very important to manage expectations. It is easy to oversell yourself. I have seen many, many interviews where people have become overconfident because the first meeting went really well.

And I have had a number of examples where at the end of the probationary period I have had to let people go, because I felt I was misled. They had pitched themselves to be so much better than their actual competence. If they had agreed the package on offer, everything would have been fine. By squeezing every last drop out of me, they had set themselves up for disappointment all round.

The same applies to job titles. Both sides can get hung up on the wording of a job title, and end up creating problems in the future. Candidates obviously pitch to be given the most senior position they can achieve, because there is status involved – but if they don't deliver at that level, if they don't perform, it will backfire. Smaller organizations are often too relaxed about the title they give people, and use it as a perk in the job negotiation. But a job title carries a perceived level of responsibility. Unless the person in the job delivers against it, the title doesn't work. Say a company gives a job function which is really that of a sales manager the title 'Sales Director' because it suits the candidate to have that on their business card; they can't then bring in somebody else to do that job. If the company grows and they do now need a proper sales director, they're stuck because there's a wrongly titled sales manager sitting in the way. Job titles need clear definitions and responsibilities. They have a specific purpose. They are not there to stroke your ego.

Finalizing the small print

You get offered the job, agree the salary and you receive a contract. It's time to move from offer negotiation to contract negotiation. How do you deal with your contract of employment? Should you just sign it? Should you use a lawyer? What are you looking for in the contract? Here are the things to look out for in employment agreements: pay reviews, termination process, gardening leave, restrictions.

In the first instance I would not call the person you will be working for, or the person who interviewed you. I would call the HR person and say, 'Thank you very much for the employment contract, which I got yesterday. Is it possible I could pop in for ten minutes and go through it with you, because I don't understand some of the points?'

Go in, sit down with the HR person, and literally turn the pages. Go through point by point, and I mean point by point. Ask them everything you can: 'What does this mean? What are the implications of that wording? What are the consequences of that clause? How will that affect me?'

Work through the perks and allowances and negotiate better terms if you can. 'I understand it's a basic salary of £50,000. Is there a company car or a car allowance? Do I get a petrol card? What about expenses, pensions, life cover, health insurance?' None of these are irrelevant points. And if you are being excluded from a particular benefit or allowance, why is that? Is it your status, your position? At what point will you qualify for it?

If the job requires a significant amount of travel, will you be flying business or economy? What is the company's policy on that? What's their position on the time you spend away from home – how does that work? The clearer the position is when you start, the less room there will be later for misunderstanding.

I would go down this route first, because it's free, and maybe at that point you don't need a lawyer, if you're comfortable and feel everything has been carefully explained.

And to be honest, if it was my company, I would respect you if I heard from the HR team that you had done that. It shows me you pay attention to detail, that you are no fool, that you do not sign just anything that's sent to you, that you're professional.

Depending on how senior the position is, I think you could, and beyond a certain level should, seek some measure of professional advice. But even then, it doesn't have to be very expensive. If you go on to the internet, there are plenty of lawyers and service agencies who offer employment advice.

Remember, once you have signed the contract, you will be bound by it. You have accepted those terms. You won't get a second chance.

Preparing for day one

You have signed the contract or the letter of agreement. But I don't think it's a good thing if, at the end of that process, nothing else happens and all of a sudden, bang, you turn up on Monday a month later. I would call the line manager and say, 'Hi, Bob, how are you? I just wanted to let you know I've accepted the position and I've handed my notice in. I'll be starting on the 14th, and I wondered if I could pop in to see you next week or the week after to talk about the role and the opportunity, and meet the other people in the team?'

I would take the initiative. You probably have some holiday owed, and you'll be winding down at your old job. Taking a day, maybe two, to go into the new company should be straightforward. Because by the time you start, the more you know and the more people you've met will make that first day, the first week, so much easier.

Bearing in mind that you're on trial, on probation, for the first three months, and everybody's watching, **what can you do to make the best impact?**

When you walk through the door, you should hit the deck running.

On that day or two you spend with a new company, double-check your gut feeling about the culture of the company. Because that's not something you can pick up fully in an hour, or from a couple of interviews. It is not something that's written down: it's an emotion, it's how you feel. A full day or two within a business, spent around the staff, in different meetings, maybe going out for lunch with somebody on your team, will give you a good sense of the culture. At the end of that you may feel, 'This is me to a T.' But equally you may feel it's not going to work out. There is still time to say no. Better to spend one day finding that out than to lose months of your life stuck in a work environment you don't enjoy.

Whatever your job function – HR, sales and marketing, finance – any time you can spend getting to know your new job in advance will pay dividends. If your job is in finance, ask to have a set of accounts that you can study before you start. If it's a sales position, can you take a look at the customer base, study the CRM system, see how the IT system works? Ask for a copy of the company's organigram, which you may not have been given at the interview stage, so you can understand how the business is put together.

At Hamilton Bradshaw we don't wait for you to call, we call you. If your job is as an investment director or investment manager, and you're going to be looking after two or three existing companies, I would bring you in and arrange for you to have lunch or meetings with the companies you're going to be looking after. I want you to be mentally prepared and raring to go.

Just as when you started the whole interview process, the better you prepare, the more you understand; you are going to come across completely differently when you walk in on day one. And the guy who appointed you is going to look like a star.

Now, go and treat yourself to that champagne, get the cupcakes in, book a table at The Fat Duck – whatever it is, **celebrate the way you enjoy most!**

A FINAL THOUGHT

I went to a doctor a year or so ago for a series of tests as part of one of those annual health checks.

When we had a review at the end of the process, I said to the consultant, 'OK, I've done all the tests now. What is your advice to me?'

All he answered was, 'I haven't really got any.'

'Oh,' I said, 'that's a bit disappointing. You're not exactly cheap, and I'd rather like to get some feedback.'

He looked calmly back at me. 'James, what do you want me to tell you that you don't already know? Shall we just go through it? Are you eating correctly?'

'No.'

'Are you exercising correctly?'

'No.'

'Are you working too hard?'

'Yes.'

'Do you eat late at night?'

'Yes.'

'I don't even have to ask you these questions,' he said. 'I can tell, because of what I see sitting in front of me, exactly the kind of life you lead. And you know the life you lead, you know you work too hard and put in too many hours. You are probably stressed like a screwball . . . which is one of the biggest factors in diseases and illnesses. But you already know all of that. What do you want me to tell you? Because whatever I say, it's not going to make any difference to you. And I'll tell you why it's not going to make a difference: because it's not important to you.' That was his killer line – 'Because it's not important to you.'

So I asked him, 'What makes you think it's not important to me?'

'Because if it was, you'd be doing it, wouldn't you?'

He was brilliant. He was deliberately provoking me and it *absolutely* did the trick, because the way he had communicated his message was that he didn't really care, because *I* was not really bothered. But if I *could* be bothered, he might want to spend some time working with me.

He was telling me that I knew all the things that I shouldn't eat, but I was still eating them. If I listened to him and didn't eat fried food, increased my intake of fruit and vegetables, didn't eat late at night, and exercised, I already knew that the chances were I would find myself in much better shape.

I followed the consultant's advice. I started working out, I ate better, I didn't eat at night. And as a result I became the fittest I'd been in ten years. I lost a lot of weight, I gained agility.

Then, because I had achieved that success, I stayed motivated, because it was working. I lost the weight, I felt better, and I wanted to maintain that good feeling about myself.

I would like you to react as I did when I heard what the doctor had to say. I want you to put this book down and act on it, to go out and transform your career and your job prospects. I don't want you to be someone who reads this and thinks, 'Oh, yes, that's all really interesting, but it's too hard, too much work. I haven't really got time to do all that preparation and planning James keeps banging on about.'

Everything in this book has drawn on my experience in the world of recruitment – that's coming up to thirty years of experience now – and I believe that each piece of advice I have given you is what you need to do in order to improve your odds of getting the job you really want. If you follow those pieces of advice, there is no question that you can change your life.
But you've got to follow them.

In the 1980s when I set up Alexander Mann, my first recruitment company, the recruitment industry was all about personality. You were successful because you had a great personality, you were sales-oriented, you were quite hungry, and that's what created success for recruitment consultants. That's the way we all operated. Some of us did well, and some of us didn't.

I happened to be in America looking at a recruitment company over there which had 600 branches. I was really shocked that in every branch I visited, they operated recruitment in a very structured and systematized manner, which

I had never seen before. They had taken the business of recruitment and turned it into a process, not a personality.

Their approach was alien to me. I had always believed that people did well because they were larger-than-life go-getters.

This company said, 'No, no, no, that's never going to work, because you can't build a business on personality. We have 600 offices. We employ 2,900 consultants. James, you will never be able to scale your business on personality.'

So, my next question was, 'But how can you do that?'

What they had done was to take the recruitment process and divide it into thirty steps. And in each of those component parts the process was very focused, incredibly detailed. I travelled all over the States visiting their branches, and was amazed that everybody I met in every office followed the process. They made sure that every step of the way, they took the trouble to do the right thing – and it worked. They were very successful.

Their message to candidates was simple: 'If you don't follow each step correctly, you have a 1 in 30 chance of getting the job. With our system we have a 100 per cent chance.'

This book follows the same principle. Before you break down the process of getting a job, you might imagine there are four steps: find the vacancy, send your CV, go for an interview, get the job. I'm saying that if that's all you do, you are missing twenty-six other key points. If you follow all the other points, you will change the odds.

I have tried to avoid filling this book with endless checklists and grids of do's and don'ts – I wanted it to be more like a mentoring session, a conversation, a dialogue. But this is the one place where I think a checklist is valuable. Here is my thirty-step process to getting the job you really want.

1 **Look at the value you are adding to your existing company: are you an asset or a liability?** Can you tangibly demonstrate the value you would bring to a new employer and prove you will be a cost worth absorbing?

2 **Define and quantify the skills, especially IT skills, that you use regularly in your particular role.** Think about the best way to explain how those skills will benefit the company interviewing you, and how they will make it more efficient and effective.

3 **Change creates opportunities, but consider the long-term impact on your life.** Make sure you are 100 per cent committed to your decision – either to change your job or career, or to stay put and transform the potential of your current job.

4 **Follow the classic business rule of finding a need and filling it.** You don't want to expend unnecessary time and energy. Channel all your efforts towards those companies that are actually going to have the job that's right for you.

5 **Use every route that's available to you:** recruitment agencies, direct applications, digital job boards, personal contacts, word of mouth – and concentrate on reaching the decision maker, the person who is going to offer you the job you want.

6 **Consider every aspect of your CV** – how you word it, the structure, the way you deliver it, the covering letter – so that you position yourself ahead of the pack by telling the potential employer you are the solution to their problem.

7 **Check that, like a good grocer, your CV puts the best apples right at the front of the stall.** Make sure every piece of information is directly relevant to the specific job you are applying for: it should be a bespoke item.

8 **Preparation, preparation, preparation. And then more preparation.** Research the company, what's going on in their industry sector, the person who's going to be interviewing you. It's easy with the internet, and absolutely fundamental. But remember, they may be researching you too . . .

9 **Use all the information you gather to provide the raw material for asking questions and raising discussion points.** It will give you enormous confidence in the interview. You don't have to memorize everything; it's the quality of the information that's important.

10 **Be proactive and confident in asking questions, getting feedback, maybe offering to work a week on spec.** Having the perfect CV doesn't prove you can do the job: in the interview a flash of passion might make all the difference.

11 **Always be prepared to answer the question, 'What do you know about our company?'** There is no excuse for drying up, floundering, waffling. Have the answer ready instantly, and then ask a question that shows you want to learn even more.

12 **Don't take any risks with your personal presentation.** Use the company's website to research their general style, and if necessary modify your look. You don't want to appear out of synch with the kind of job you would be doing.

13 **Have a checklist in mind, so you can go through every single aspect of the way you come across** – from clothes, hair, fingernails, to your briefcase or bag, how you shake hands, how you sit. It's all in the detail.

14 **As soon as you meet your interviewer, work hard to connect with them straight away on a personal level** by finding an ice-breaking remark, or asking a question about a photo on their desk or an award on the wall in reception.

15 **Make sure you get in with an early question**, ideally one that asks the interviewer to tell you what they consider the key components of the job. This will give you the perfect agenda to present against.

16 **It's always useful to bring something you have prepared in advance** – a short presentation, a document, something that demonstrates the quality of the work you do – but don't oversell it. Let the interviewer discover for themselves how good you are.

17 **During the interview aim to ask the interviewer as many questions about the job and the company as they are asking you.** You are trying to maintain a balance of power. The interview should be a two-way dialogue, not an inquisition.

18 **Plan ahead for the standard questions you will always be asked** – such as, 'Why do you want to leave your current employer?' – so that you don't need to worry about those and can respond naturally and confidently to any unexpected questions.

19 **Don't worry unduly about showing nerves: they prove you really want the job.** A little dash of self-deprecating humour can help relax the mood. Be upbeat, friendly, show you would fit in – and maybe send a thank-you note afterwards.

20 **Practise answering killer questions in advance, so you have an original, relevant answer**, and try to avoid the trite tactic of immediately asking a question back. Work out what lies behind each question: what does the interviewer really want to know?

21 **If you are fazed, take some time out.** The easiest way is to ask if you can use the bathroom, which gives you vital time to reprogramme and reposition yourself, so you can return to the interview back on track.

22 **Ask if you could come in and meet the department before a second interview:** the knowledge you'll gain will make you stronger at the next stage – but don't lower your guard, especially if you're invited to a 'matey' night out.

23 **Try and get a feel for the company's culture while you are in the building, and ask questions to find out more about it** – you want to know if this is a place you feel you could actually enjoy working in.

24 **I always say that the real skill lies in the questions, not in the answers.** Have the courage to ask questions that might come back with a negative answer. Your bravery in asking tough questions will not go unnoticed.

25 **Don't forget to get feedback at the end of any interview.** Remember that little line you can use as you are escorted to the lifts, 'What's your gut feeling?' You'll always learn something that will be valuable to you.

26 **Keep professional right up until you have left the building.** Only relax once you are completely out of sight and out of earshot. You don't want to blow your chances at the last moment with an unwise remark.

27 **Always learn from your mistakes.** If a job interview doesn't work out, go back to the company and find out the reason why, so you can draw something from the experience and improve your performance next time you apply for a job.

28 **When you are offered a job, step back to take a calm, collected view of what is on offer** – and it still is only an offer – before negotiating a deal that is fair for both parties. Seek professional advice if necessary.

29 **Take care when you are choosing who to provide as your referees**, and be courteous enough to tell them in advance that they may get a call from your potential employer: you don't want any surprises at the final hurdle.

30 **During the first days, weeks and months after starting the job you really want, you're still on trial.** Hit the deck running: listen, learn and contribute. You'll make the person who appointed you look great, and you'll feel great too.

Now when you look at each element of the process, none of it is rocket science. It's all common sense. But there is a lot that can go wrong. It is the detail, the minutiae, that makes the difference. And it really is astonishing how few people can be bothered to make the difference. I think that ego often gets in the way. People believe they are instinctively brilliant at selling themselves, but the truth is most of us are not skilled at that. We have not been trained to do it. We have never been given that advice. We have to learn how to do it. And we have not been motivated to learn. I want you to be motivated not only to learn but to put what you have learned into practice.

If at any point you need a moment of motivation, just ask yourself: do you want to be part of the crowd, or do you want to be the person who rises above the rest?

Do you want to be in the lottery, or do you want to have the winning ticket?

This book is your winning ticket. Don't lose it.

Acknowledgements

First and foremost, I would like to say a big thank you to Lucy Heskins, whose feedback and comments have been invaluable throughout this journey. I also want to thank all of the people who have contributed to this book, including Joel Rickett and everybody at Penguin, Jonny Geller and the Curtis Brown team, David Head at Recruitment International, Helen Reynolds at HB RIDA, Tony Seager at Seal-RTS, Ian Wolter at Eden Brown, Phil Roebuck at Webrecruit and Bev James at the Entrepreneurs' and Business Academy.

I would also like to thank Philip Dodd for his help and dedication in translating hours of my thoughts into a fantastic and coherent book.

In addition, I would like to thank my dedicated team at Hamilton Bradshaw – all of whom have helped make the process as efficient as possible – with a special thank you to Sally Poinsette.

Lastly, I would like to thank my loving family, who have always fully supported my 24/7 workaholic lifestyle, allowing me to fulfil my aspirations for changing the way recruitment is delivered in this country and enabling me to gain the experience necessary to write this book.

Appendix
Using the Power of the Web

The big, big change in the recruitment business over the past few years has been the way in which both candidates and employers have tapped into the phenomenal power of the internet. Online activity is now a major part of any job-search strategy. I'm often asked if I can give some advice on the most useful websites, so here is a selection of sites I'd definitely recommend taking a look at.

For careers advice in general, your first port of call should be the government's own site, **http://careersadvice.direct.gov.uk/**. This site is a practical starting point, whether you're looking to change careers, need some tips on developing your skills, or help on completing application forms.

Another general advice site I'm always recommending, to graduates in particular, is **www.careerplayer.com**. If you're looking for a resource that provides support every step of the way, from discovering what career you'd like to pursue to tackling curve-ball interview questions, this site is definitely worth a visit. Also make sure you check out their psychometric questions section.

Milkround (**www.milkround.com**) is another great site for graduates and people looking to secure jobs and internships. And the Prospects site (**www.prospects.ac.uk**) is fantastic if you're researching a particular sector and want an insight into salaries, working conditions and much more.

There are plenty of free websites dedicated to writing the perfect CV: each one has a different take on how to craft it, so spend time searching for a site that's appropriate for your chosen sector. If you want to use the services of professional CV writers, try speaking to the guys at The CV Store (**www.thecvstore.net**) or the team at Concept CV (**www.conceptcv.co.uk**).

Two sites that specialize in using digital video technology to present your CV in an innovative way are Talent on View (**www.talentonview.com**) and CVSeeMe (**www.cvseeme.com**).

In terms of general, multi-sector job boards, Jobsite (**www.jobsite.co.uk**), Monster (**www.monster.co.uk** and **www.monster.com**) and Totaljobs (**www.totaljobs.com**) are three examples of the big boards out there – make sure you carry out a targeted search for positions in your area. They all offer good advice on interview techniques.

In addition to the multi-sector job boards, you should focus on the industry-specific boards. These sites cater for virtually every sector, so I'll pick out just a few key areas. If you work in IT, you can upload your CV on to the Jobserve website (**www.jobserve.co.uk**). If you're in sales, I'd suggest visiting the Sales Target site at **www.salestarget.co.uk**, and I don't need to tell you which career you're in if you go to JustEngineers (**www.justengineers.net**). For senior-level, executive appointments you should include The Ladders (**www.theladders.co.uk**) as part of your search.

There has been a surge in online recruitment agencies offering a fantastic range of services to job seekers. If you're looking to register your CV with the experts within this area, make sure to use Webrecruit's service: **www.webrecruit.co.uk**. They use the Web to source candidates for employers who don't know which job board is best for their needs.

An interesting site for women who are looking for specialized advice, jobs in all sectors and positions offering flexible working is Working Mums (**www.workingmums.co.uk**).

And finally, if you're looking for a one-stop shop offering the details of the UK's recruitment consultants, Agency Central (**www.agencycentral.co.uk**) is definitely worth a visit. Aimed at both job seekers and employers, it offers a comprehensive directory of details and covers a multitude of sectors.

Remember, these are just a few examples and should serve purely as a basic platform for your job search. The job market is going to get even more competitive, so putting in the extra research is a given. Make sure you maintain your momentum and stay passionate, and your hard work will pay off.

BILL JENSEN AND JOSH KLEIN

HACKING WORK: Breaking Stupid Rules for Smart Results

It would be so much easier to do great work if not for pointless bureaucracies, outdated technologies and deeply irrational rules. These things are killing us. Frustrating? Hell, yes.

But take heart. Today's top performers are taking matters into their own hands: bypassing sacred structures, using forbidden tools, and ignoring silly corporate edicts. In other words, they are hacking work to increase their efficiency and job satisfaction.

In this groundbreaking book, consultant Bill Jensen and hacker Josh Klein reveal how to work smarter instead of harder. Once you learn how to hack work, you'll accomplish more in less time. You'll cut through red tape and circumvent stupid procedures.

Hacking Work is about making the system work for you, so you can take control of your workload, increase your productivity, and help your company succeed – in spite of itself.

One of *Harvard Business Review*'s Ten Breakthrough Ideas for 2010

'Not for the meek, *Hacking Work* is for those who truly want to change the way they do business' Marshall Goldsmith, author of the *New York Times* bestsellers *MOJO* and *What Got You Here Won't Get You There*

PHILIP DELVES BROUGHTON

WHAT THEY TEACH YOU AT HARVARD BUSINESS SCHOOL

What *do* they teach you at Harvard Business School?

Graduates of Harvard Business School run many of the world's biggest and most influential banks, companies and countries. But what kind of person does it take to succeed at HBS? And would you want to be one of them?

For anyone who has ever wondered what goes on behind Harvard Business School's hallowed walls, Philip Delves Broughton's hilarious and enlightening account of his experiences on its prestigious MBA programme provides an extraordinary glimpse into a world of case-study conundrums, guest lectures, *Apprentice*-style tasks, booze luging, burn-outs and high flyers.

And with HBS alumni heading the very global governments, financial institutions and FTSE 500 companies whose reckless love of deregulation and debt got us into so much trouble, Delves Broughton discovers where HBS really adds value – and where it falls disturbingly short.

'Delves Broughton captures an essence of HBS that is part cult, part psychological morass, part hothouse . . . His book is invaluable. Quite brilliant'
Simon Heffer, *Literary Review*

'A funny and revealing insider's view . . . his fascination is infectious' *Sunday Times*

'A particularly absorbing and entertaining read' *Financial Times*

'Horrifying and very funny . . . An excellent book' *Wall Street Journal*

GREGORY ZUCKERMAN

THE GREATEST TRADE EVER

Autumn 2008. The world's finances collapse – but one man makes a killing.

John Paulson, a softly spoken hedge-fund manager who still took the bus to work, seemed unlikely to stake his career on one big gamble. But he did – and *The Greatest Trade Ever* is the story of how he realised that the sub-prime housing bubble was going to burst, making $15 billion for his fund and more than $4 billion for himself in a single year. It's a tale of folly and wizardry, individual brilliance versus institutional stupidity.

John Paulson made the biggest winning bet in history. And this tells how he did it.

'Simply terrific. Easily the best of the post-crash financial books' Malcolm Gladwell

'The definitive account of a sensational trade' Michael Lewis, author of *Liar's Poker*

'Extraordinary, excellent' *Observer*

'A great page-turner and a great illuminator of the market's crash'
John Helyar, author of *Barbarians at the Gate*

'A must-read for anyone fascinated by financial madness' *Mail on Sunday*

'A forensic, read-in-one-sitting book' *Sunday Times*

BOB BURG & JOHN DAVID MANN

THE GO-GIVER: A Little Story about a Powerful Business Idea

The Go-Giver tells the story of an ambitious young man named Joe who yearns for success. Joe is a true go-getter, though sometimes he feels as if the harder and faster he works, the further away his goals seem to be.

One day, desperate to land a big deal at the end of a bad quarter, he seeks advice from the enigmatic Pindar, a legendary consultant referred to by his devotees simply as the Chairman. Over the next week, Pindar introduces Joe to a series of 'go-givers' who teach Joe how to open himself up to the power of giving.

'Most people don't have the guts to buy this book, never mind the will to follow through and actually use it. But you do. And I'm certain that you'll be glad you did' Seth Godin, author of *The Dip*

'Not since *Who Moved My Cheese?* have I enjoyed a parable as much as this. You owe it to yourself to read *The Go-Giver* and share its message with those who matter most to you' David Bach, author of *The Automatic Millionaire*

'*The Go-Giver* is the best business parable since *The Greatest Salesman in the World* and *The One-Minute Manager*' Pat Williams, author of *Souls of Steel*, and senior vice president, Orlando Magic

STUART DIAMOND

GETTING MORE: How to Negotiate to Succeed in Work and Life

You're always negotiating. Whether making a business deal, talking to friends, booking a holiday or even driving a car, negotiation is going on: it's the basic form of all human interaction. And most of us are terrible at it.

Experts tell us to negotiate as if we live in a rational world. But people can be angry, fearful and irrational. To achieve your goals you have to be able to deal with the unpredictable.

In Getting More, negotiation expert Stuart Diamond reveals the real secrets behind getting more in any negotiation – whatever more means to you.

Stuart Diamond is the world's leading negotiator. He runs the most popular course at Wharton Business School, advises companies and governments on conflict resolution, and is the man who settled the Hollywood Writers' Strike.

'Practical, immediately applicable and highly effective' Evan Wittenberg, Head of Global Leadership Development, Google

'I rely on Stuart Diamond's negotiation tools every day' Christian Hernandez, Head of International Business Development, Facebook

'The world's best negotiator' City AM